GETTING RICH
YOUR OWN WAY

SRULLY BLOTNICK, PH.D.

D1440710

PLAYBOY
PAPERBACKS

The author's research, upon which this book is based,
was funded in part by the National Science Foundation.

GETTING RICH YOUR OWN WAY

Copyright © 1980 by Srully Blotnick

Cover photo copyright © 1982 by PEI Books, Inc.

Published simultaneously in the United States and Canada by Playboy Paperbacks, New
York, New York. Printed in the United States of America. Library of Congress Catalog
Card Number: 81-86252. Reprinted by arrangement with Doubleday & Company.

Books are available at quantity discounts for promotional and industrial use. For further
information, write to Premium Sales, Playboy Paperbacks, 1633 Broadway, New York,
New York 10019.

ISBN: 0-867-21130-X

First Playboy Paperbacks printing August 1982.

10 9 8 7 6 5 4 3 2 1

Contents

CONTENTS

PART ONE

CHAPTER ONE

Who Becomes Rich, and Why?

Everyone wants to be rich. Some people want to be millionaires just to *be* millionaires, others want to be wealthy so they can stop worrying about unpaid bills and upcoming expenses.

Chronically high rates of inflation and a huge tax bite seem to be standing in the way. Yet the fact remains that, in spite of all the obstacles, some people make it. Who they are, and why they became millionaires, are what this book is about.

We started out with 1,500 people who, in 1960, represented a cross section of middle-class America. Since the United States is now and has always been a predominantly middle-class country, that is the group we wanted to focus upon. The vast majority lived in cities or suburbs. We lost almost a third of them along the way, due to death, moves to parts unknown, or simple refusal to respond to any more of our follow-up inquiries. Of the 1,057 who remain two decades later, 83 have become millionaires. What is amazing is that all 83 appear to have become rich accidentally.

Our aim in this book is to improve significantly your chances of having a similar accident. It may sound strange that we want you to have an accident. The word usually means a bad rather than a good one. Yet that does indeed have to be the goal, and for a very important reason.

Everyone we talked to who wanted to become rich was able to tell us how it could happen, if only . . . They could spell out what would first have to occur, what major and minor changes would be needed in their daily lives, for fame and fortune to subsequently come knocking on their door.

They were being realistic, they felt, because they had a plan. They might not have been able to tell anyone else how to become rich, but they knew exactly how they themselves could get there. "If I moved to ——," or, "If I were willing to do . . ." mounds of cash would automatically be theirs.

Why, then, didn't they do it? Because they were unwilling, they said, to put themselves through so much pain and discomfort "just for the money." They had a problem: they wanted to be rich. And they also had the solution: a plan which would have brought them a fortune had they decided to put it into effect.

We've been carefully examining those plans and schemes, hopes and dreams, for the last twenty years. Some of the people we followed attempted to push and shove, scratch and claw their way to the top. Others used a less openly aggressive, but more devious approach. Some tried one field, others tried another. Many sought their fortune through gambles and bets, hunts for buried treasure, and what they hoped would be spectacularly profitable investments.

Yet, not one person who had a plan for becoming rich was able to successfully carry it out. The plan, it turned out, worked against the planner. Although having a blueprint before you begin is absolutely necessary in certain activities—for example, constructing a building or bridge—it only hampers, rather than helps you become rich.

The most widely shared impression we found was that great wealth can come to you only as a result of doing things you don't want to do. Most were aware that if they worked harder they could earn more. Logically, then, they felt that if they worked constantly and frenetically, especially at work they hated, they would inevitably become rich.

Like so many other thoughts about "how to get rich," it sounds reasonable and is flatly contradicted by the evidence. In fact, if you don't like your job, you are losing money. Lots of it. Because as it turns out, your work is more likely to make you wealthy than any bet or investment you will ever make.

The crucial role played by work you enjoy is only one of the startling conclusions which emerged. There were others. Socializing, for instance, isn't likely to help make you rich, and may even lessen the odds of its happening. It may be great fun, and glamorous too, but in almost every instance it made the road to fame and fortune longer, not shorter.

Competitive feelings turned out to be less useful than everyone originally thought. Competition is an integral part of our lives, and we expected the most competitive people to be the most successful. They weren't. In fact, although we heard more (and more often) from the rival rabbits, it was the tortoises—more intrigued by their work than what their competitors were doing—who were the clear victors in the race for riches.

From the start, most of the people in our sample assumed that chance would play a decisive role in determining who became rich. The very thought tickled their fancy and got them quite excited. After all, if making a fortune was merely a matter of luck, then it could just as easily happen to them as to the next person. Someone else became rich this year, but who knows? Next year, they might be the one.

Something all were convinced of is that "the rich are not different from you and me." They believed it strongly, and even angrily. And they turned out to be right. There were many brilliant, talented, dedicated, and energetic people who didn't do well financially in spite of having tried hard for over twenty years. Edison's famous comment, "Genius is 10 percent inspiration and 90 percent perspiration," doesn't apply very well to the financial sphere. Neither inspiration nor perspiration proved to be enough to make someone wealthy, no matter what proportion of each existed.

A missing ingredient, a key one which operates so quietly it has previously been overlooked, had to be present if someone was ever to become rich: they had to find their work absorbing. Involving. Enthralling. The words sound dramatic, yet what they refer to is tiny in everyday terms, and nearly silent. But those who eventually became rich had it, and those who failed did not.

What are some of the characteristics shared by people who became rich? Here are five.

First, they were persistent.

Although they, like everyone else, were fond of doing a variety of things, it was the fact that they picked a field or activity and stuck with it, through good times and bad, which finally allowed it to make them wealthy. They knew it, too. Because once they became wealthy and were asked how they got that way, they usually replied without hesitation that it was persistence which was responsible for their success.

Second, they were patient.

We all want to be rewarded instantly for what we do. It doesn't seem fair to have to work hard and wait forever for our efforts to bear fruit. Yet, impatience prevented many from making it.

In fact, it sometimes seemed that those who ultimately were successful were willing to wait forever, if necessary, for the rewards of the labors to come to them. Strangely enough, that is obviously what it takes: if you are waiting restlessly for your first million to arrive soon, the odds are good that it won't ever arrive.

Third, they were willing to handle both the nobler and the pettier aspects of their job.

Much as we'd all like to avoid "dirty work," it is clear that we often can't. There are always a host of trivial details and minor tasks which we may wind up having to take care of ourselves.

It was interesting to see that those who eventually became

rich didn't think *anything* connected with their work was "beneath" them. To be sure, there were some parts of their job they liked much more than others. But if need be, they were willing to do them all. And often had to.

Fourth, as time went by, they had an increasingly noncompetitive attitude toward the people with whom they worked.

Kids in school are very competitive. They can't help it. They are constantly being compared to all the other youngsters in their class. "Who is taller, prettier, stronger, sexier, and smarter?" are questions they can't avoid.

But as high school becomes an increasingly distant part of the past, it is apparently quite important to leave behind you the attitudes which prevailed there. What characterized outstandingly successful people is that, with each passing year, they became less and less competitive. They were interested in what others around them were doing, but did not allow themselves to be blindly guided by it. They had their own particular interests. And while they kept an eye on everyone else's approach, they pretty much went their own way.

Fifth, their investment activities consumed a minimum of their time and attention.

We originally expected the people in our sample to become wealthy by taking the money they earned at work and investing it wisely, in such things as stocks, bonds, and real estate. We had intentionally excluded the children of wealthy parents from our study, since they were going to inherit wealth rather than have to make it on their own. So we thought there'd be no way for the people we were following to become rich unless they used their surplus income to generate more income.

We expected that to take up a lot of their time. After all, you can't be completely ignorant about real estate and securities and still hope to do well. You need to know a certain amount merely to make a transaction.

Learning about the major fields of investing, staying informed about current market tastes and changes, not to mention the tax aspects of each transaction, had to be time-consuming. We thus anticipated that the wealthier someone became, the more of an amateur stock or real estate broker they'd become. Their knowledge would, we thought, increase with the value of their assets.

It didn't work out that way. We were surprised, to say the least, to see how haphazardly they handled their investment monies. Rarely did they buy the most profitable stocks or buildings. In fact, forgetting for a moment the money they made at their work, their investment results were remarkably mediocre. More often than not they made little or no money investing. Frequently they wound up taking a loss.

That was a real eye-opener. Because it let us see with stunning clarity what the actual source of their wealth was: their work. In case after case, they did increasingly well occupationally, while their pursuit of investment profits proved to be largely a waste of time. In the long run, it was their work—and only their work—which made them rich.

They didn't know that. They too thought their investments were going to make them millionaires. Thus the wealthier someone became, the guiltier they felt about not tending to their investments. They repeatedly made comments such as, "I ought to be subdividing the land I own and selling off building plots"; "I'm not getting as much rental income as I should from my vacation home"; "I should spend more time watching my stocks," and, "I think I'm letting too much of my money just sit in savings accounts." As it turned out, they worried much and did little. In spite of their guilty feelings, they fortunately seemed to unconsciously know where their chances of financial success were greatest.

We need to say a few words here about lies. When money is the subject of conversation, lying is common. But what hurt the people we studied far more than the false statements they made to others were the falsehoods others told them. The most damaging of the lot were comments people made about how easy it was for them to make all the money they now allegedly had.

We all envy someone who appears to have a genuine knack

for making money. Books and magazine articles abound, written by people claiming to have made themselves rich, quickly and easily. And now that they have found and refined the perfect method, it can be yours for a modest price.

Regardless of what they would have you believe, it turns out that in most cases their secret scheme not only didn't work for them, it won't work for you, either. In those instances where someone did indeed make a great deal of money quickly, they usually lost it just as quickly. Easy come, easy go. But all you ever hear about is the first part—and then, only after they've had a chance to distort it considerably. Nevertheless, at least for a while, they are able to convince hordes of money-hungry followers that they know the route to the pot of gold at the end of the rainbow. As one put it, "I'm not doing much harm. I only take a little bit from each."

In a way, that is true. Because there are many more amateur liars than there are professional ones. Not only are there more of them, they are far more lethal to your financial health. At least with the pros, you know you're being sold a bill of goods, and hence you are likely to defend yourself with cynicism, questions, and a sudden fondness for keeping your hands in your pockets.

On the other hand, when your friends start stretching the truth about how rich they are (they don't have to use words to do it), you are much more likely to be taken in by it. Your guard is usually down at the time and it tends to stay down, since they are merely conveying the facts about their finances. Without realizing why, you may find yourself feeling somewhat inadequate. Obviously, there is something wrong with you. If it is so easy for the people you know to make money, it should be just as easy for you.

In an astonishing number of instances, we had the distressing opportunity to watch someone lie through their teeth to a friend about how much money they had or were making. Trying to keep up with someone you know who is doing well is hard enough. Attempting to match a fantasy they are spinning for you may make you give up in despair. All we can say is: don't. The fact that you've known someone for years doesn't mean they won't tell you some of the most outrageous financial fictions you will ever hear.

By now you've probably guessed that this book is going to be very different from other investing books. We aren't going to tell you how to turn the small change in your pocket or purse into a small fortune. Only people trying to sell you lottery tickets want you to believe it happens every day. Nor are we going to tell you how to beat the ponies, the market, or the casinos. There are probably wild speculations of all kinds that have paid off. But the people we studied didn't find any, although they searched high and low. There is no question about it: it certainly would be nice to go from rags to riches overnight. I wish I could tell you how to do it. Better still, I wish you could tell me.

However they got there, once the people we followed became wealthy their lives often changed drastically. They began to become public figures, whether they liked it or not. They were asked to join a variety of clubs and organizations, to serve as members of committees and boards, or make generous donations to the institutions of which they were now a part. Their wealth and position made them useful to people who were trying to raise money or whose activities needed someone to lend them an air of respectability. Quite frequently, the wealthy went along with it. But the cultural and charitable festivities created a somewhat bizarre image in the public's mind.

In fact, the rich and famous generally socialize so often, everyone now thinks that socializing is what made them rich and famous in the first place. Our results show, however, that hanging around with people who are wealthy and well known, assuming you can get to do it at all, isn't particularly useful. You may as well hang around in a bank, hoping your pockets will somehow become full. Besides, standing around in a bank won't cost you anything, but you could easily go broke trying to keep up with the stars.

Speaking of the stars, at the conclusion of the study we interviewed over 200 multimillionaires. Their average age was fifty-four and their total personal net worth exceeded $7 billion—an average of $32 million per person. Although each knew of the study, none knew its conclusions. Their words are their own. The comments they made, which appear throughout the book, were a result of their being asked by us to identify the factors they felt had been critical to their success.

You may be wondering why a psychologist would be so interested in who becomes rich, and why. It won't come as news to you that poverty makes people unhappy. It has been romanticized in certain novels and movies, but when people are given a choice, they don't choose to be poor.

Those who are middle-class and are struggling to make enough just to break even are also subject to a considerable degree of strain. At some point, the complaints people voice cease to be a psychological matter and instead become a financial one. Where is the crucial dividing line?

Anyone who has a problem involving both emotions and money isn't going to be helped by someone saying to them, "I'm a specialist. Only your personal problems matter to me. The financial ones are *your* headache." We live in an economy now, even more than we do a community. And no amount of anti-business bias can erase the fact that money plays a major role in our lives.

Throughout this study, we were particularly interested in discovering how much we could find out about someone by seeing what they did with their money. How they earned it, spent it, worried about it, and viewed it turned out to be immensely revealing. Very little of real importance happened to them which did not, in one way or another, involve money.

That enabled us to have conversations which would otherwise have been impossible to even start. There are people who don't want to think about, much less discuss, the sexual or family difficulties they are having. But they are happy to talk endlessly about their financial dealings and woes. They see money as impersonal, though we now know it is anything but.

Moreover, they have the mistaken impression that their financial lives are simple and straightforward, and hence a serious attempt should be made to present them that way. They have the equally mistaken impression that their personal lives are enormously complex, and hence no effort to understand what is going on can possibly succeed.

Their willingness to discuss the former, and their reluctance to delve into the latter, are based on an inaccurate view. False though it may be, it nevertheless nearly forces them to try to think clearly about what they are doing financially, and why. That is very fortunate, because what they do with their money is as revealing as what they do in bed. In fact, it's more so.

That the world affects the way we feel about ourselves no one doubts. The financial difficulties each of us encounters are clearly capable of upsetting us. But the reverse of that is true and is fascinating, as well: Our personal problems often have a major impact on how well or poorly we do financially.

There are all the ingredients needed here for a devastating downward spiral to begin: a small emotional kink may produce a moderate problem at work which then magnifies the size of our personal troubles. Round and round they go, lower each time, until a point is reached at which it is no longer useful or feasible to separate the two. They have to be understood and treated together.

It is no longer enough for us to understand what someone is like on a desert island or in a Garden of Eden. We also need to know what they are like in the disturbing and prolonged heat of a business context. Perhaps it is unfortunate that most of us have to work, but the fact remains that we do have to. And with work now occupying so large and significant a place in our lives, it has become enormously more important for each of us to understand any and every contribution we happen to be making to our own occupational, and hence personal, downfall. Nothing is more distressing than to yearn and strive for success and then have it never arrive, thanks to our unwittingly having been our own worst enemies all along.

There is an upward as well as downward spiral. In this book, we are going to see what happened to people who were well matched to the activities in which they became involved and whose earnings soared as a result. It isn't true, of course, that people who had no personal problems were successful and those who were troubled failed. Indeed, some of the craziest people we studied became the wealthiest.

The fact that they were somewhat off the wall didn't prevent them from becoming some of the best snake oil peddlers imaginable. The dedication with which they conducted their business was a sight to see. And it proved expensive to anyone who happened to have the misfortune to do business with them. Since these characters were indeed a breed apart, we've given them a place of their own, in Chapter Nine.

Leaving the crazies aside for the moment, there was one area of conflict which kept surfacing repeatedly. The couples we talked to frequently told us that one of the major sources of dispute they had was money. In many instances, they appeared to be right. The financial styles of the two partners did seem to clash. Sometimes the distance between the way in which two people handled and thought about money looked too large to bridge.

We didn't know it when we first started examining people's financial lives, but some solid conclusions we hadn't been looking for about this subject slowly emerged. Although the dominant theme of the pages you are about to read is "what it takes to get rich," they should also help significantly to better your personal relations, particularly if your partner's spending style turns out to be distinctly different from your own.

Nothing you read here is likely to change the way you or your partner approach financial matters of an everyday sort. But the way you view that difference turns out to be far more important than the difference itself. And your view of the difference is indeed likely to change as a result of the chapters to come. As we'll see, even a minor shift in your attitude can produce a sizable improvement in the quality of your relationships.

A final note. Anyone who tells you that this is a book about work, instead of money, has missed the point entirely. All we originally wanted to do was see who becomes rich, and why. As long as it was legal, frankly we didn't care if they made their fortune on a street corner with a tin cup, a monkey, and an organ or did it by figuring out how to break the bank at Las Vegas.

In fact, we intentionally did not exclude from our sample a large number of people whose occupations or hobbies seemed at the beginning of our study to stand no chance of ever becoming anything but a pleasant pastime.

Conversely, for the last twenty years we have paid particularly close attention to anyone who seemed to have found a valid way to "get rich quick." It would have pleased us no end—not to mention the profit we would have made—had we found even one such scheme. We started out with no prejudices in this area and tried to remain as open-minded as we could from start to finish. Anything anybody came up with that could be proved to produce a fortune, not just for them but for anyone who used it, was of interest to us. However, that had to be the criterion. The fact that someone won a million dollars in a lottery, say, doesn't mean you ever will, no matter how many tickets you can realistically buy and no matter how many years you spend buying them. What is of monumental importance here is this: the fact that it succeeded for them does not mean that it will be a successful route for you.

As the years passed, we were shocked to see who was becoming wealthy and who was not. We initially had thought of people's jobs as offering them prestige, an interesting if somewhat frustrating way to spend the day, and finally, some money, if not a great deal of it. We had no way of knowing in the beginning how important work people enjoyed would turn out to be for ultimately making them rich.

If you are anything like the people we studied, you're having enough difficulty making a decent living as it is. We are not going to make matters worse by telling you we've found a secret formula that will make you rich overnight. There is no such thing, though we know plenty of people who've gone broke looking for it. What we are about to describe might be labeled a "get rich slow" technique. But it works. And nothing else does. In fact, it offers the largest number of people the financial—and personal—rewards they want.

It is now clear that the world of work has enormously more room for additional millionaires than does the world of investing. People who strike it rich in stocks, bonds, real estate or commodities are so rare, they usually attain some notoriety. On the other hand, it is an everyday occurrence for people to become wealthy as a result of their everyday work. It happens so often, it almost never results in a headline.

The wildly disproportionate attention given to those who've made fortunes investing deceives us mightily. For it makes us think that we should be trying to do the same. Leaving behind us the huge work arena in which our chances of becoming a millionaire are at their peak, we thus enter the relatively tiny investment arena where we'll be lucky merely to break even, much less grow rich.

For the vast majority, it is a one-way trip. Having made the journey, they never return. That is highly unfortunate, because as it turns out, they've turned their backs on the best and most satisfying opportunity to attain fame and fortune they'll ever have.

CHAPTER TWO

How You Get Paid, and Why It Matters

Dave is fifty pounds overweight, but it doesn't slow him down at all when he is trying to make a sale. With his mouth and arms moving nonstop, he inundates you with his message. His enthusiasm is infectious, and it is clear that he believes everything he says.

"You've never seen office space this good, at these kinds of prices. The place is light and airy, with great views in every direction." The customers listen and nod, though they may as well not be present. For once Dave begins his heated description, he becomes so caught up in what he is saying he no longer needs listeners. "These rooms, they're just the right size," he comments to no one in particular.

Although he is forty-two, his round face and straight hair, parted neatly, give him a youthful appearance. His complexion is light and his skin doesn't tan, it burns. His face is usually red, but it's hard to tell whether that is due to his having been in the sun too long or his excitement about the prospect of a rental or sale.

By anyone's standards, his spending is impulsive. He devotes less thought than most to his purchases, and when he is asked, "Why did you buy so-and-so?" he is at a loss for words. It is one of the few times he is.

His free-wheeling approach to spending has a flip side: he loves to wheel and deal at work. Free of rigid guidelines, a foreigner to meticulousness, he is at his best when talking in terms of vague generalities and images of broad scope. "I'm good at pulling all the pieces—and people—together," he is fond of saying. And it is true. His record of earnings as a real estate salesman confirms the fact that for all the hysterical handwaving he does, he earns a sizable sum of money in commissions each year.

Starting with $8,600 his first year in the business, his annual earnings over the last twenty years have mushroomed rapidly, if unevenly, to their present level of over $170,000. Nevertheless, he hasn't got a dime in the bank. Over the years, he has taken in a great deal of money. And spent every last penny of it.

Why is that so important? Because we are less interested in how much someone earned than how much they kept. If all they did was act as a conduit through which hundreds of thousands of dollars flowed, then we can only say, "Hope you had a good time." For we are going to give center stage to people who eventually became wealthy.

That doesn't mean you are seventeen pages into reading a manual for misers. Hoarding every last cent is much less likely to make you rich than you might at first imagine. The evidence unmistakably indicates that you have to spend money in order to make money. However, one question which we will later examine turns out to be crucial. Namely, what to spend the money on?

Before discussing Dave further, let's look at Susan. Although they are strangers, her spending pattern too seems to compel her to rid herself of any money she has. The oldest of four children of hard-working parents who firmly believed, "A penny saved is a penny earned," Susan considers saving absurd. "When I shop," she says blithely, "I'm doing some good for the economy, creating employment."

Susan makes commercials for a living. Her early dream was to become successful in acting, a field she now characterizes as "full of bitchy and backstabbing people." It provided her barely enough income to live on: an average of $4,625 per year in the beginning.

In the past sixteen years, she has spent an increasing portion of her time auditioning for commercials, instead of parts in plays, and her income has soared. For the last three years, she has earned an average of $109,000 per annum. While she still thinks occasionally about acting, and as she puts it, "probably wouldn't refuse a part in a major motion picture if it were offered to me," for the most part she has "left all that behind me."

She and Dave earn money in clumps, and spend it the same way. That's not unusual. We found that, regardless of income bracket, someone whose earnings arrive sporadically, but in big pieces, is likely to spend it without much thought.

It was fascinating, however, to discover that the reverse was also true, and was far more significant. Someone who spent money haphazardly and unthinkingly usually wound up fifteen years later in an occupation which was unlikely to pay them neat, regular amounts.

It had finally become clear which was the chicken and which the egg. Right after finishing college, most postwar youngsters found jobs which paid them a steady salary. Nevertheless, it was precisely those who spent their money impulsively who tended to end up ten to twenty years later working for commissions, fees, or being self-employed.

They had strong—but unconscious—feelings about the way in which they wanted to disburse whatever money they had. And slowly but surely as the years went by, they managed to organize their work lives so that the money came in the same way in which it was going out.

It is easy to see why Susan's and Dave's many friends, who watched with growing envy and awe as the annual amounts the two earned rose, couldn't imitate them. Let Susan's classmate, Betty, who is also in our sample, tell it to you in her own words.

After going to an endless number of auditions, and even landing a few parts in commercials, Betty quit: "The one thing that kept getting on my nerves was the uncertainty. You never knew from one week to the next whether or not you'd be working."

That's true, as far as it goes. But in addition, it meant that Betty couldn't be certain paychecks would be arriving regularly. To her, that is no minor matter. She likes paying her bills promptly, and wants to always have enough money in the bank, so that, as she puts it, "I don't have to lose sleep worrying about it." Above all, she dislikes going into debt, and makes little use of the charge cards she has. Although she deeply wanted to follow in Susan's footsteps, it never really represented a serious possibility.

In Betty's view, Susan is "a gambler"; "willing to stick her neck out." Yet, as Susan saw it, what she was doing was merely "going after the only kind of work I really like."

Dave's friends and co-workers were hampered by similar difficulties in attempting to copy him, something many were tempted to try. They considered the work he was doing outrageously easy, and were amazed that he was being paid such a substantial sum for doing it.

No one squawked louder than Ed, a longtime acquaintance of Dave's. Yet Ed's efforts along similar lines came to naught. His ability to wheel and deal turned out to be limited, because he automatically found himself considering a transaction from every conceivable angle. Its pros and cons, its details and consequences, were factors he couldn't easily overlook. Unfortunately, while he was busy examining every aspect of a pending deal, the potential parties to it wandered off. His many fine qualities were clearly not being put to their best possible use as an imitator of Dave.

Ed has always been a careful and deliberate shopper. And although over the years he regularly told us how happy he'd be to make a speculative "killing," he, unlike Dave, soon stopped devoting his entire day to attempting to make that happen. In fact, given the choice, he almost always selected positions which offered a guaranteed income of moderate size rather than one with a theoretically huge payoff, which might, however, never be seen.

AGONIZING ABOUT MONEY

When our long-term study of the role money played in people's lives first began, we knew that the amount of agonizing someone did about it would prove to be important. Little did we realize at the time just how important it would turn out to be.

The agony index, as we called it, simply measured the amount of time taken and agonizing done by an individual before, during, and after a purchase or sale. Some, particularly impulsive people, scored a solid zero: they took little or no time to make up their minds about what to buy, and didn't worry about it in the least, neither then nor later. Others, conversely, thought and agonized endlessly, and wound up with a score which went right off the top of the scale. In fact, some are still kicking and second-guessing themselves now, twenty years later, for decisions they made then.

The glad-handed spenders in the first group and the tightfisted ones in the second were not present in equal numbers. Of the 1,057 we studied, 202 (approximately 19 percent) were like Susan and Dave. On the other hand, 562 (about 53 percent) were like Betty and Ed. The remaining 293 (28 percent) agonized somewhat when buying or selling, but not much, and took time to make up their minds, but not a great deal. Nevertheless, the latter two groups envied the former one quite a bit.

What makes that strange is that they had less to envy than they realized. The situation is analagous to one we encountered when interviewing people about sex. There were a number of married couples who were having intercourse an average of three times a week, who were envious of what they thought was the sex-every-night pace of the people they labeled "swinging singles." However, the people so labeled were actually having sex a little less than half as often as the married couples were. Having a regular partner conveniently close by typically increases the frequency of intercourse. By contrast, many of the swinging singles told us they spent more time looking than finding.

As with sex, so with money in this instance. The regular paychecks being received by the majority of wage earners may not have seemed like much. Yet over the years, they added up to more in total earnings than those who collected large amounts, though only sporadically. In fact, Betty and Ed have received almost 37 percent more in total lifetime income than Susan and Dave have. And thanks to the stop-and-start character of their work, there is good reason to believe that that gap will widen rather than narrow in the coming years.

What *is* different—and obviously very appealing—is the size of the sum which Susan and Dave occasionally receive. Most of the people we studied want the best of both possible worlds: the paycheck they currently get, together with a spectacular windfall at irregular intervals.

That's not likely to happen, since Susan and Dave, on the one hand, and Betty and Ed, on the other, represent entirely different work-styles (which are far more fundamental than life-styles, and not nearly as modifiable).

It is clear that when people say, "I like my job," they often mean that, in addition to the work, they like the way in which they are paid. The word "work" has come to serve as a euphemism for "money." In some ways that's appropriate, since, as we've seen, more important than the amount of money people now earn is the pattern of payment they receive for doing it.

In short, it took years, but most people ultimately managed to make their earning pattern match their spending pattern. They frequently commented, "If I had more to spend, I'd spend more." Yet without realizing it, they eventually chose jobs which gave them the income pattern—not the amount—they found most satisfactory.

A sizable portion of the working population, however, is not matched to the income pattern they'd find most satisfying. In the next section, we'll see why.

MISMATCHES

Alan, age thirty-nine, wants to be rich. As a youngster he loved tinkering, taking things apart and solving problems. As naturally as birds take flight, he drifted into engineering, and after graduation went to work for a large electronics firm.

Ever since he was old enough to understand what his parents were talking about, he heard them in essence saying, "Money solves all problems." Even when they said the reverse, he could tell they didn't mean it. He grew up considering money the equivalent of a fountain of youth, and since he felt himself to be growing old fast, he wanted desperately to find it. "I'm twenty-six," he said three years after leaving school with his Master's degree, "and I still haven't made it big."

As soon as he began work, his interest in engineering was overrun by a financial focus which soon came to dominate it. A careful spender, Alan thus pushed himself out of research (at one company) and into sales (at another) because, as he put it, "That's where the big money is." Forcing himself to move further in the High Roller direction at first wasn't easy. But in time, he came to like it.

The fact that he was being paid in a different way—commissions instead of a salary—had a variety of effects which he overlooked, and one he did not. "Now," he boasted, "I stand a good chance of *really* raking it in."

Thirteen years have passed. And although his income has certainly increased (to $48,000) since he began in his sales position (at $12,600), he hasn't yet reached the point at which he finally feels he is "raking it in" in the desired quantities.

The contrary, in fact, seems to be the case. The many factors and uncertainties which go into the calculation of his paycheck frustrate and irritate him. So much so, that although he is making more now, he is clearly enjoying it less.

More than the fluctuations in the size of the twice monthly checks he receives, what disturbs him are the doubts and delays. If a customer doesn't pay (or pays late), Alan doesn't get paid (or is paid late). "I have expenses to cover," he snaps, "and I'm never sure I'm going to be able to."

Since it has slowly but surely become clear to him that he isn't about to become rich as a salesman, he has been devoting an increasing portion of his hopes and energies to investment activities which he pursues outside the office.

Carol, thirty-eight, also found herself pulled toward being a High Roller. But it wasn't high hopes which drew her in that direction. It was Barbara, her old roommate. The two had originally majored in art in college, but unable to support themselves after graduation in their field, they moved to a major city nearby and started looking for jobs.

Unlike Carol, who is extremely tightfisted, Barbara spends freely and easily. After two and a half years of holding low-salaried positions as a sales clerk in a few prestigious department stores, Barbara decided to go into business for herself. "The salaries were a joke," she quipped at the time, "and barely covered my cab fare to and from work." Laughing, she added, "No matter what I do, I won't make less than I am now." With Barbara providing the organizational vision and Carol the labor, the two opened a jewelry-manufacturing business selling to stores.

Their designs were original and well executed, and within a year they had gathered a sizable volume of orders. They needed and found larger living-and-working quarters and were just able to shoulder the increased overhead they now had, thanks to the increased volume of business they were doing.

It was then that the crucial differences between them, which had been sitting just beneath the surface, began to emerge.

Given her cautious spending tendencies, Carol would have liked nothing better than a guaranteed, and steadily rising, salary. Yet she *believed*—believed in the quality of their work and the business they were building based upon it, and she believed in Barbara, who possessed all the drive and promotional skills required to make the vision she repeatedly described come true.

Had the business been larger and more profitable, Carol could have arranged to receive the pattern of payment she preferred. As it was, with their sales volume good at certain times and no orders whatsoever to process at others, she was exposed to a degree of variation in her income which she found nerve-wracking.

On several occasions, when business was particularly poor, she asked, "Where will we get the money we need for rent and food?" The distress wasn't shared by Barbara, who found Carol's constant complaints both puzzling and irritating. "I only know," she said cynically but seriously, "that the money always comes in, one way or another. Worrying about it is a waste of time." Armed with that belief, Barbara could shoulder levels of debt which, more than once, made Carol wake up in the middle of the night in a cold sweat.

After fourteen years of ups and downs, they split up. Although Barbara had unwittingly tried to see to it that Carol got the stable pattern of payment she needed ("I always get paid last," Barbara said comfortably, a comment Carol could only have made angrily, if at all), it wasn't enough. Carol was finally fed up with the continual uncertainty, while Barbara was fed up with trying to pacify Carol instead of pitching for new business.

Carol now works for a salary, and is visibly less tense. "It's peaceful," she says of her job, "even though it will never make me rich." Barbara, on the other hand, remained in business for herself—"I could never work for one of the large corporations," is a comment she frequently makes—and has prospered.

Let us look at another typical example.

Larry is a hardworking and highly competent physician. Although he is one of the most careful spenders we studied, one who repeatedly scrutinizes every potential purchase, and then does so again after the transaction has been concluded, he too found himself drawn toward the High Roller end of the spectrum. However, no one was pulling him in that direction. As with everything else in his life, it was only after much deliberation that he finally decided to consciously make the move.

What caused Larry to act were calculations he had made. They showed conclusively that he could make a lot more money being self-employed and collecting from each patient ("fee for service") than he could with a salary, regardless of the number of patients served.

His income wound up being high, but so was his level of dissatisfaction. It annoyed him that he had to wait so long to get paid. And in many cases, he was able to collect little or none of the fee. Still, he knew he had made the right decision in organizing his work life the way he had. Financially, if not emotionally, the arrangement was sound.

MORE THAN A PAYCHECK

Although a wide variety of people thus are drawn toward the High Roller end of the spectrum, an even larger number are pulled in the opposite direction: they work for salaries, but they'd rather not.

Ted, for instance, is thirty-six, and unfortunately, no salary he is able to realistically earn matches his free-spending inclinations. Impatient, as he put it, "with the irrelevance of school," and wanting "to get on with living," he dropped out of college after his second year.

Even though it frustrates him, he has spent the last sixteen years—since he dropped out of college at twenty—collecting a salary. His parents were people of modest means, and with four children to support, they were unable to bankroll any of his plans for the companies he wanted to start. Nor could he accumulate the seed capital he needed by working, since his loose grip on money kept getting in the way. Whatever he made, he quickly and easily spent.

Since he lacked any lucratively employable skills, the jobs he did get came to him because he was personable, funny, and totally honest. More than once, and without the least fear of being caught, he could have pocketed money and products which weren't his, yet he would never have even thought to do so.

Employers valued those qualities, but not enough to make him a manager of or partner in their business. With most of his talents still undeveloped, such an action would have smacked of charity, in their minds. And thus far at least, we haven't met anyone who'd consider Ted's past bosses reasonable, much less charitable. What's left, as Ted puts it, is that "I work in a Holiday Inn, but I'd rather own one."

Since he doesn't own it, though, he can (and does) take it all lightly. Much as he'd like to be self-employed, he is aware that a good part of his everyday enjoyment depends on others being saddled with the real headaches. Even so, he still has a lot of good ideas for businesses. Maybe one day, if he forces himself to put away some money, he might even try making one of his schemes a reality. That does seem a less likely prospect with every passing year.

Unlike Ted, Janet, who is forty-one, has both the training and experience needed to go into business for herself. She also has access to the required capital, either from her parents, who are comfortable, if not wealthy, or from others she has worked with in the past, who would be willing to back her now.

Janet's spending is relaxed at best and impulsive at worst. Neither before, during, nor after a purchase does she experience more than a modicum of concern. Her attitude is simple: "If I spend, I always make enough later to cover it."

She works best under pressure, she says—and without realizing it, earns best under pressure as well. As with more than half the people we studied, it is by spending that she generates the additional pressure she needs to help keep herself totally immersed in her work. And since there seem to be a large number of things she wants ("something new each season"), she isn't about to run out of supplementary motivation.

Her involvement with her work is deep, and after starting at twenty-one as a sales clerk, at $4,700, she recently became the general merchandise manager of the large chain of stores for which she works. Thanks to a steady series of raises during the period, her income—currently at $100,000—has managed to stay ahead of her expenditures, and as a result, she has rarely been heavily in debt.

It was only when the rapid rise in her income slowed that her appetite for self-employment grew. She is now in process of establishing her own company.

As with many others we studied, it was only when her pay approached a ceiling—and hence her financial future became certain—that her interest in running a firm of her own surfaced. The majority of High Rollers in Janet's position had been toying with the idea for years, and now that, as they put it, their "hands were tied" and their "options so limited," they were ready to act on the idea. They usually claimed it was "independence" that they were seeking.

Perhaps. But it is illuminating to note that, although they had considered starting a business of their own for years, they did so primarily when they were angry, or else when they wanted a chance to make an unspecified amount of money.

Anger automatically makes people think about independence. But opening their own business would give them a chance at something they noticed less, yet wanted more: a source of speculative income.

For some people, antiques, gold, real estate, and stock market investments offered that possibility—and they often searched frantically for a way to make "a killing in the market." Others, though, wanted an active business rather than a passive investment—and thought endlessly about companies they could found which would make them "God only knows how much money."

Both, however, wanted the same thing: a random—and they hoped, lucrative—pattern of payment. Those who were receiving a steady paycheck but who dreamed of an investment making them rich wanted it less. Without realizing it, they liked the stability the salary they were collecting provided.

On the other hand, those who were going into business for themselves wanted a variable income more than part-time investors did, and were willing to devote themselves full time to finding it. Indeed, they were usually willing to take a substantial earnings cut in order to have that opportunity.

In fact, tallying the results for the last twenty years, and taking account of the large number of small businesses they owned which failed, it emerged that those who worked for large corporations made approximately 32 percent more in total income during the period than did those who were self-employed.

In spite of that fact, those who owned their own businesses thought they were far ahead of the corporate employees in the income race. Even after they'd seen the proof that they weren't, few seriously considered changing their working lives. What it boils down to is this: they weren't in it just for the money, although they repeatedly said they were.

If their income came to them in regular doses and they spent it irregularly, it simply wasn't sufficiently satisfying. When all is said and done, *how* they got paid was far more important than *how much* they got paid.

Regardless of their strong inclination to leave, many of the highest of the High Rollers we studied stayed put at the major firms which employed them. Part of the reason they stayed was that, in many cases, the pay was good. For example, John Bullis, Senior Vice-President at Saks Fifth Avenue, told us that high salaries were by no means rare, and that, in fact, more than half of Saks' forty Vice-Presidents are only between the ages of thirty and thirty-nine and currently earn "a minimum of $50,000, up into the six figures."

Bullis, intent upon attracting to Saks the best retailing talent he can find, thinks that people in a hurry to open their own small store are doing themselves no favor. "It's a difficult business," he said, "and the experience you gain at a large retailer will help you substantially, when and if you later decide to go on your own."

"Besides," he added, "the knowledge you gain in your own small store isn't of much use to a major retailer. We hire a number of such people, as assistant buyers and department managers, but they have to take a real step backward in terms of pay. In a large operation like ours, you need to be familiar with management, merchandising, finance, and distribution, on a scale which exceeds anything you can pick up in a small store."

Dan, age forty-four, provides a typical example of what usually happened to the people in our sample. A division manager at a cosmetics firm, he is often annoyed at "all the nonsense that goes on in this place," and comments acidly, "If I owned this firm, half these nitwits would be out on their butts."

Nevertheless, he hasn't taken any concrete steps toward opening his own company, and isn't likely to, either. For all the complaining he does—and he does a great deal—it's not the cut in income he'd have to take, at least initially, which prevents him from leaving.

As he sees it, it is laziness, instead. "I guess I'm just a big talker," he has stated more than once. If he is, so are countless others who, like Dan, are High Rollers raring to go, but who in fact aren't going anywhere.

"Here I don't have to keep dredging up new business," commented one, who works for a well-known ad agency. "Someone else has to. Pitching for additional clients isn't for me." Large firms have a large number of employees—"too many," was the opinion of some—and hence there is always someone available to attend to every aspect of the business being transacted.

However, "When you're on your own," said a High Rolling friend of Dan's who had started a business which subsequently failed, "you're *really* on your own. I couldn't afford
to hire all the people I needed, and had to do everything
myself—sales, shipping, and sweeping the floor."

FEELING RICH

Others made similar comments. On any number of occasions
people told us, "I just don't know how to make money," and,
"I'm not good at it." And to some extent, that was true. There
are indeed tips and techniques which, once learned, can increase your earnings minimally. Also, as pointed out by John
Bullis at Saks, and by many others as well, it turns out to be
quite important to know a fair amount about the business you
are about to start. A hasty entrance was usually followed by
an equally speedy exit.

Nevertheless, for some reason, most of the people in our
sample felt it was a lack of determination, not knowledge,
which made them remain at the firms which employed them.
Since their situation was, as they put it, "comfortable, if not
exciting," they lacked the motivation to leave. As High
Rollers, their spending was fitful and somewhat careless, yet
they liked the fact that regardless of what they did—short of
being fired—their paycheck would soon magically appear. It
made some of them giddy at times: "I don't know whether I
earned it or not, but I'm glad it's here."

In sum, almost everyone who works has one chief gripe: "I
simply don't earn enough money." So many people say it so
often, it is undeniably true, in part. But only in part. The
culprit, it tells us, is money. "As soon as I get a raise, my troubles will be over." However, it doesn't take many years of
studying a large group of people, all of whom earn the same
amount and have the same living expenses, to realize that everyone looks at money very differently.

More importantly, they spend it differently. Three people

who are given the same amount to spend might spend it flamboyantly, thoughtfully, or very reluctantly. We call the three, respectively, High, Low, or No Rollers, but it is really a spectrum and there are people at every point on it.

How they spend is interesting, but how their spending affects the rest of their lives is crucial. Over a period of years, most people unconsciously try to arrange their work lives so that it will provide them with a pattern of payment which matches their spending tendencies.

They do indeed try, but still it often doesn't. In fact, approximately 45 percent of the people we studied were mismatched, and in one way or another they knew it. It bothered some considerably. Others, however, weren't bothered enough to do anything about it. Either way, the mismatch between what they had and what they wanted continually made itself felt. Depending upon how actively they wished to be involved, they either dreamed of starting a sensational business or else of making a spectacularly profitable investment.

Many wanted very much to do something about their high level of dissatisfaction, but didn't know what to do. Not having a clear idea of the problem, they were unable to come up with a helpful solution. If that applies to you, this book should be of real use—even if you don't intend to make any changes in your working life.

It is valuable to know why something disturbs you even if you can't, or don't want to, do anything about it. And the mismatch we've been discussing will indeed disturb you.

Why? Because it will prevent you from feeling rich. Few things are more illuminating than to watch how differently people react when the same amount of money (say, $20,000) is given to all of them, but is given to all of them in different ways. Those who receive a pattern of payment which matches their emotional spending pattern feel richer. In fact, they think they are earning more even when they are earning less. It *feels* right to them, and that above all is what registers.

CHAPTER THREE

Accidental Investing

If all people did was eventually match their inflow to their outflow, they'd merely break even. The process might be fascinating for us to watch, but it certainly wouldn't make the people doing it rich. For that to happen, some part of their income has to remain theirs.

Surprisingly, those who already felt financially comfortable, as a result of a good match between how they received money and how they were inclined to spend it, were far more likely than others to ultimately become wealthy. To see why, let's look at a few examples.

Paul, now forty-six, finally realized in his late thirties that he couldn't save his way to being rich. His paychecks were large, but his overhead was larger. A moderately High Roller, the $54,000 salary he received as a production supervisor at a chemical company seemed to flee from his fingers. The result: he was never able to accumulate any funds for investment.

Since his paychecks weren't going to get him there and he couldn't save enough to even get started, he felt compelled to gamble. Repeatedly he said, "You have to take chances." Every time he got his hands on a small clump of money—anything from $1,500 to $12,000—he'd "take a shot." Sometimes it was in the stock market (primarily the computer, gambling, or gold stocks), other times it was in Las Vegas or the neighborhood race track.

Occasionally he'd win. And when he did, he considered his repeated attempts to "hit the jackpot" justified. Rather than being out of the ordinary, he considered a winning bet or profitable play a sure sign that more of the same would soon happen.

It rarely did. In fact, he usually lost substantially more than he won. Since most of his losses were small (and easily forgotten), whereas the times he won loomed large in his mind, he thought that over the years he had "just about broken even." His judgment is apparently somewhat clouded in this area, since his actual losses over the last sixteen years total approximately $121,000.

Phil, too, gambles. And loses. But he claims that it is the excitement he wants, even more than the profit. He doesn't overlook the losses, but considers them to some extent an entertainment expense.

A bright forty-one-year-old industrial fabrics salesman, his travels bring him in contact with a wider variety of situations he can hope to profit from than those Paul encounters. Phil not only plays the ponies and the hot stocks, he also speculates in land and condominiums "for a quick turnover." "In and out," he says. "I want to be there early—or first—and then get out when the suckers start arriving in crowds."

It hasn't quite worked out that way. The land he bought from a developer he paid taxes on each year, and during that time the $19,000 he had invested earned no interest. After holding the parcel for six years and selling it for $20,000, when he decided to buy some gold bullion instead, he felt he had done all right. "Not bad. I made $1,000."

It had been his intention to hold the land for six weeks, not six years. But he was unable to find a "Johnny-come-lately sucker" who was willing to pay him more for the land than he himself had paid. If he had put his money in the bank, at say 8 percent, his $19,000 would have earned him almost $10,000 in interest. In addition, he paid almost $4,000 in taxes on his land during the six years. In short, he didn't make $1,000, he lost $13,000. But no matter, as he is quick to point out, "It's not over yet. There'll be a next time."

Martha, age thirty-nine, is in public relations, and as she will happily tell you, "Sooner or later, I am going to be rich." A High Roller of the first order, whatever money comes to her she has long since spent. Although she earns $37,000 a year, her salary seems to her "a mere pittance." "God knows," she says, "it doesn't go very far." Nor does it take very long for her to send it on its way.

"I'm not going to wait forever for it to happen, either," is another of her favorite phrases, one she often utters as she buys a state lottery ticket, something she does almost automatically with any small change she has in her bag.

Her best friend, Clare, is quite knowledgeable about horses, having grown up on a farm which bred them. Every once in a while Clare comes up with a horse or jockey she considers worthy of note. The two women then bet—either with their friendly neighborhood bookie or else at the race track—Clare in a small way, Martha in more sizable amounts, sometimes as much as $400 per race. "It's been fun," Martha comments, "but that's about it."

She has also tried her hand at investing in jewelry and antiques. But the evidence indicates that she knows as much about either as Phil knows about vacant land and condos.

She is solidly convinced that the rings, pendants, pins, paintings, mugs, platters, and chairs she has bought from time to time are worth a small fortune. But an independent appraisal valued them at one-fifteenth the price she assigned the collection: $5,000, instead of $75,000. "I wouldn't sell any of them," she has stated flatly. "One day, they'll be priceless." Here's hoping. After all, she has spent over $43,000 on the stuff.

What Paul, Phil, and Martha have in common (along with hundreds of others in our sample) is this: they are impatient.

They don't want to be wealthy when they're old. They'd like to find their fortune soon. Maybe even tomorrow.

Before we discuss the important effects impatience has, we first need to gain some understanding of the cause of the impatience.

There are undoubtedly a large number of factors contributing to someone's momentarily being in a hurry. Maybe they've got to go to the bathroom, or they are hungry or annoyed. But if instead of watching people for a few moments we study them for years, two factors causing their financial impatience emerge as being the most important.

First is the question of how well matched people are to the pattern of payment they are receiving. And second, how much do they enjoy the work they are doing, in exchange for that pattern of payment?

THE PRESSURE TO BECOME RICH

People who aren't matched to their preferred pattern of payment will know that something isn't right, even if they can't specify what it is. One way they'll know is that they'll feel they aren't being paid enough, no matter how much they are being paid. High Rollers generally don't see a salary—*any* salary—as adequate compensation for the work they are doing. And conversely, Low and No Rollers don't like the uncertainty which comes with receiving varying paychecks at varying times.

Some people don't care about becoming rich. But if you do, the fact that you don't *feel* adequately paid will probably make you try harder to earn more money. In some cases, that will be no tragedy. It may cause you to work longer and more diligently, and hence later result in an increase in your earnings.

Yet, bizarre as this may sound to you, the overwhelming majority of people we studied were already trying much too hard to become rich.

"How can that be?" you might wonder. "How can anyone try *too* hard to make money?" That is a question we've been asked many times, by genuinely puzzled people, and we can best answer it by asking you to consider a different version of the question. Namely: If you are someone who wants to become rich, how long do you expect it to take?

A week? A year? Two, three, or five years? Or ten, twenty, or even thirty years?

Pick one.

We didn't know it two decades ago, when we began this study, but it turns out that the shorter a time period people chose, the less likely they were to become rich.

Why? Because almost without exception they devoted themselves to making "a fast buck." Those who were looking for quick turnovers and instant profits were powerfully inclined to buy things which glittered but were usually worthless.

In short, the faster you expect your fortune to arrive, the more likely you are to lose whatever money you already have. Or will have.

What Paul, Phil, and Martha—and the millions like them—did was to constantly search for schemes, gambles, and the pot of gold at the end of the rainbow. The only people who made a sizable sum were the ones who were *taking* their money. All told, the three threw away a twenty-year total of $306,000. Ironically, they had spent that sum trying to find a way to become wealthy.

By the way, is it your guess that any of the people we studied became rich overnight as a result of breaking the bank at a casino, a spectacular play in the stock market, a lucky lottery ticket, or a long shot at the track?

We wish they had. There are indeed million-dollar winners in the lottery, but there weren't any among the people we followed. Some of ours were lucky enough to be big winners in the market, or at the casino or track, on one day. But they gave it back—and then some—on another. Much as we'd have liked to see a sudden fortune materialize, it didn't happen. Not once.

Be that as it may, there was one astonishing characteristic shared by everyone who became worth $1 million or more: they didn't notice how wealthy they had become. Basically, it crept up on them.

It was interesting to compare the responses they had given over the years to the question, "When do you expect to become rich?" with that given by people who hadn't done well. The most common reply given by those who had fared poorly was, "Any day, now," whereas those who'd become rich usually answered with, "I don't know." And they really *didn't* know: they were too busy with what they enjoyed doing to spend much time monitoring daily their own net asset value.

Some comment is required here about the word "enjoy." When we say that someone enjoyed their work, we don't mean that they were thrilled to death every minute to be doing it. If the quantity of conscious happiness people experienced and the amount of visible joy they demonstrated were the criteria we'd been using for whether or not people liked doing something, we'd have had to quickly conclude that no one enjoys the work they do.

Early on, it became clear that another approach was needed, one which focused on how absorbing people found their work. Many told us, "I don't enjoy what I do," but if it caught them up and kept them involved year in and year out, their actions spoke louder than their words. Moreover, if they thought one hour of work had taken them twenty to forty minutes, we took that as a further indication of their involvement.

ENJOYMENT

You might watch a sporting event for hours on end, and be filled with anxiety and distress every minute of that time, concerned about how well your struggling team is doing. If you said, "It is painful to watch," but were riveted to what you were seeing, for our purposes we'd have to say you enjoyed it. Junkies don't like dope; they just need it.

And it was precisely work which someone personally felt the need to do which eventually made them rich. Why? Because they did enough of it, and for sufficiently many years, so that they became good at it—very—even if they never once said they liked it.

Bill and Alan Anixter, who started a wire and cable manufacturing and distribution company in 1957 with $10,000, now do over a quarter of a billion dollars of business a year. Their company's stock is traded on the New York Stock Exchange. Alan, the President of the firm, told us:

"Some people said we succeeded because we were smart. But that wasn't the most important thing. It never is. We did well because we were willing to work longer hours than our competitors were—and we were busy when they weren't working at all.

"Saturdays, for instance, we'd sometimes spend the whole day in our car, driving to different locations to inspect and buy materials. We never resented doing it, not even for a moment.

"We wouldn't have been willing to do it just for the money, or to beat out our competitors. We've watched lots of people try, and it doesn't work. Money was their goal, and they didn't succeed.

"Focusing on money prevents everything else from falling into place. Build a good business—the money will come along as a result.

"It's funny. We didn't even notice that we had become millionaires—and we don't even know exactly what we're worth now. We've lived by a simple rule: If you don't enjoy your business, get out of it."

"I hate this business," commented Bob, one of the people in our sample, but that hasn't stopped him from staying with it for over twenty-two years. Selling cars is what he has done ever since he was twenty. Now, at forty-two, he has become remarkably skilled at what he does. "I could do it in my sleep," he yawns, to underline the point, but it is no idle boast.

Every step in the process has been perfected—from the way he greets customers (friendly, but not overly so—"People are suspicious of backslappers now," he says) to the technical details he spouts ("Not too many. People get confused."), to the relaxed and seemingly indifferent way in which he firmly guides you through the paper work which finalizes the sale. It is only after you watch his competitors for a while that you come to realize just how slick he is. Every superfluous gesture or comment has been eliminated; every grimace or line that works has been retained.

After six years in the business, he was doing well enough to be offered a small piece (3 percent) of the firm, as an inducement to stay. He had already decided upon leaving, but the offer changed his mind. Five years later, one of the owners died. A moderately High Roller, Bob, then thirty-one, was given the chance to buy another 35 percent, and did so in stages over the next four years, by taking a smaller than normal share of commissions and profits.

All the while, the firm was growing, and in the decade after the partner's death its sales and profits more than tripled. From one and a half city blocks, they expanded to four blocks of new and used cars, and then trucks. They also added a lucrative line of Japanese imports. With Bob's partner reaching sixty and looking to retire, the two were receptive to a bid from a firm which wanted to buy their land and their franchise. A deal was concluded, and Bob's share came to $775,000. As he put it at the time, "I didn't know it was worth that much." Eight months ago he used the money he'd received from the sale to start a dealership of his own (in the same GM models he previously sold) in another state.

Wendy's situation is similar. Although she spent two and a half years in college majoring in English, she had no idea what she wanted to be. After a couple of brief and boring secretarial jobs, she went to hairdressing school and definitely became hooked. At twenty-three she began working in a large salon and started to develop a following.

Outgoing and energetic, she found it easy to spend all day on her feet, talking to one customer after another "and not get all their stories—and kids—mixed up." A moderately High Roller ("I don't like thinking about what I buy," she has said, but does so a bit, anyway), she kept dreaming about having a place of her own. With strong encouragement from some of her regulars—two, in particular—she rented a small shop in a well-located, older building and at twenty-seven was on her own.

It seemed forever before business picked up. And at one point, her finances strained to the limit, she considered closing. "I think I jumped too fast," she said grimly. "I tend to do that, you know." But after ten months of shaky going, things started looking up and business began an upward spiral which lasted for years.

Initially she had one assistant, but two years later had four. Her decision to cut men's as well as women's hair was a natural one, and a host of young couples started showing up together. A year later she rented the remainder of the first floor, and a year after that, the second floor as well. Her staff had expanded to eighteen, and more than once Wendy stated that she felt overextended. "What would happen if business dried up?" she asked after renewing her lease. "This is such a faddish business. One day they love you; the next, they don't." It was a reasonable concern, but one which proved unnecessary, for her volume of customers steadily grew.

Finally, she decided to buy the building. "All that rent is going down the drain," she commented. Yet, what motivated her as much, if not more, were the memories she had of the furious disagreements her prior boss and his landlord used to have. For $75,000 *as is* (the contract stated), it was hers. And a headache it was.

The repairs, improvements, and general maintenance were an undeniable nuisance, yet while she felt like throwing in the towel any number of times, she stayed. Much of what she was earning "is going into this goddamn building," she fumed, "and it's not even my home." In some sense, though, it was.

For nine years, between the ages of thirty-five and forty-four, business grew, but at a slower pace. Whatever income she derived from the salon which wasn't needed for the upkeep of the building or the business she quickly spent. "I like nice things," she said, and hence her bank balance during this period remained close to zero.

When she was forty-one, she was offered $240,000 for the building. It amazed her. "I've owned this wreck for nearly ten years, and I didn't think it was even worth what I paid for it." Eighteen months later, the bidder was back. No specific offer was made this time, but it was interesting to see how wedded to the business she was. For all the complaints she had voiced, and all the promises she had made to "close the doors forever, tomorrow," she wasn't interested in budging.

Good thing, too. Because eight months after that, the bidder returned in earnest. "How much would it take to make you sell?" he inquired softly. "A million dollars," she joked. "That high I can't go," he said, "but I'm willing to pay you $900,000."

Wendy was stunned. And sometimes still is, when driving past the modern office building which covers the entire block on which her old shop was once located. Her new shop, three blocks away, costs her a modest monthly rent and is smaller and more attractive than the previous one was. "It's a wonderful place," she says.

You might be tempted to conclude at this point that neither Bob nor Wendy became millionaires as a result of their occupation. Their real success, you might feel, was in real estate. And on the surface at least, the conclusion is valid.

In that case, however, others who invested in real estate should have done equally well. And after examining large numbers of instances, it becomes quite clear that they did not. Surprisingly, those who, like Bob and Wendy, had *un*intentionally invested, did significantly better than investors who were looking to make a speculative profit.

How come?

For one thing, the speculators almost always sold too soon. Len and Eleanor, for example, also owned a building on the block which was demolished. Indeed, they bought the property anticipating that that would occur. Having noticed new construction activity in the neighborhood, they reasoned that it would soon encompass the building they chose.

They were distressed, however, when nothing subsequently happened. For twenty-six months they held on to the building. And fretted. Not only did they not receive any inquiries about the property, when they tried to sell it they also found no interested buyers. "No one even wanted to come and look at it," said Eleanor. "It *did* need a lot of work."

The man who visited Wendy was employed by one of the nation's largest banks, which was acting as an agent in the site assembly for a client, a major corporation. When he first visited Len and Eleanor, he made no offer, but did get an "asking price" of $400,000 from them. They had paid $265,000, which together with the taxes, overhead, and repairs (the building was largely rented, but was running at a loss), brought its current cost to approximately $305,000.

A few months later he returned, and the deal was closed for the $400,000 they had asked. They were thrilled. "We did very well," Eleanor declared.

And so they did. But in a subsequent conversation we had with the bidder from the bank, he told us that he had been authorized to pay up to $1.2 million for the property.

The example is typical of hundreds we encountered. And the sheer quantity of such instances call into serious question the very way in which the overwhelming majority of people attempt to become rich.

IMPATIENCE

It would be easy to point to impatience as the chief culprit here. After all, if Len and Eleanor had held on longer, they'd have done enormously better.

However, making people generally more patient is difficult. Making investors be more patient is impossible. It is apparently a contradiction in terms. By definition, investors have a certain amount of money tied up, and they want the money back, with a substantial profit, at the earliest possible date.

Every extra day they have to wait for a particular amount of profit, the less profitable (in real terms) their investment will have been. Therefore, if you are somehow successful in making them bide their time, they automatically proceed to raise their expectations of the percentage profit they are due.

They aren't being excessively greedy, either. Quantity and time are two fundamental aspects of any investment. It's only natural for the person to ask, "How much will I make?", and, "How soon will I get it?"

At some point then, having waited long enough, investors start becoming content with *any* profit they have—assuming, that is, they have some. Nevertheless, as expensive as impatience usually turned out to be, it can't be the whole story.

For if we focus upon only the patient investors in our study, they still did not do as well as the accidental investors did. In fact, those who in essence weren't investing at all—at least not consciously—did more than three times as well as those who invested patiently.

The reason is that the two groups chose entirely different types of investments. For instance, where real estate was concerned, what type of investment do you think investors selected? They of course chose land or buildings which were likely to appreciate in value. And what kind of investments do you think accidental investors made? They, on the other hand, chose whatever furthered the progress of the work they enjoyed doing.

A brief example will make clear what typically occurred.

After graduating from a well-known art institute, Hank decided to travel for a few years, and finally came to rest in New York. The size of the canvases he produced grew larger and larger, until he at last decided to move into a commercially zoned section of Manhattan where, above all, he'd have space. Not much else, though; no nearby supermarkets, Laundromats, or other services. But space he did indeed have: 50 by 100 feet, 5,000 feet in all. It was 1962, and Hank at the time was twenty-five. Two other artist friends reluctantly joined him in the building, because as one put it, "It's so cheap, it's almost free."

And sleazy. It was often necessary to step over bums sleeping in the doorway, and garbage everywhere piled high. Yet it served the two painters' and one sculptor's purposes admirably. The landlord died in 1963, and for a small amount of cash his wife was only too happy to unload the building. Fearful of being evicted from what he considered an outstanding place in which to work, Hank got his upper-middle-class parents to lend him the money and co-sign the mortgage. Including legal fees and closing costs, the initial outlay came to $8,800.

Very few of the real estate investors we studied would even have considered the area. Most simply thought we were joking when we asked them about investing in such locations. Of the five who did invest in the neighborhood in the subsequent fourteen years ("I must be crazy," said one. "I'll leave it to my children," said another. "By then it will be worth something."), none held out longer than six years. "It will take forever," said a third, after disposing of his holding, "for that neighborhood to become popular."

Well, needless to say, it didn't take forever. And Hank sold the building a couple of years ago for a profit of $357,000 to a High Rolling investor from New Jersey who told us, "This area is just beginning to get hot."

Maybe. But it was the fact that the area was already hot which drew him to it in the first place. If that investor is at all like the ones we studied, he'll grow tired of the property long before it appreciates very much in value. Telling him to be patient is a waste of words. When we asked him if he'd be willing to hold on to the building for sixteen years—as Hank did—he just laughed. "Are you kidding?" he commented. "I'm going to double my money, and be out of here, in two."

It's been two years. And you probably won't be surprised

to discover that he is still there. And worse, the highest bid he has been able to get thus far for the building is the price he himself paid.

We're certainly not suggesting that our results show artists, hairdressers, and car dealers to be better at buying real estate than serious investors are. But what is clear now is that people who were simply doing work they enjoyed and, thanks to the enjoyment, persisted in that activity, reaped two monumentally important rewards:

First, they were patient. It was accidental patience, but patience nonetheless. It doesn't matter how it got there; it's the end result which counts. They weren't continually saying to themselves, "Slow down"; "Stay calm"; "Don't sell to the first bidder," yet they acted in a manner which allowed their investment to finally attain its potential, instead of getting rid of it far too soon.

Second, and of equal if not greater importance, accidental investors tended to buy things which hadn't yet become popular. As a result, they were there long before the crowds came. Sometimes, of course, the crowds never did come, but that was OK, too; they hadn't bought the item with that outcome foremost in their minds.

Intentional investors, on the other hand, were almost always mesmerized by something which began to become fashionable. In fact, it was only when something became hot—that is, popular with speculators—that they finally viewed it as a good place to invest their money. Almost without exception they underestimated the number of people ahead of them in line; they thought they were among the first, when they were actually among the last.

One statistic which emerged tells the story in a particularly revealing way. Until now, it may have seemed that there were two separate and distinct groups—one of accidental, the other of intentional investors. And as we shall see later, to some extent that was true. But if we restrict our focus to the accidental investing the intentional investors did, we find something remarkable.

The largest investment speculatively oriented investors accidentally made was the purchase of their own home. Sure, the investment value of the place mattered to them, and some talked about little else. Yet, other considerations mattered far more: its location, appearance, whether they liked the color, materials, and look of it, etc. Basically, they bought it because they liked it.

That wasn't the way in which they approached the houses they bought for strictly speculative purposes—that is, ones they purchased not to live in but to resell. There they bought because (they hoped or assumed) others would like it.

Key question: On which house do you think they made more money?

Actually, it wasn't even close. They made approximately 106 percent more profit on average on the houses they had bought as *un*intentional investments—and they were able to live there, as well, an additional profit we've not included.

A final note. As we mentioned previously, it was striking to see that people who became millionaires rarely even noticed it. It snuck up on them while they were busily involved in the activity they found so absorbing. Not only did they not notice it, they were truly reluctant millionaires. Few leaped to sell the building or business which had earned them their fortune. But that's precisely the point: had they been nervously watching and waiting for the magic, million-dollar figure to arrive, they'd have wound up selling long before it had.

In short, there are two, crucial stages. People who became millionaires were *not* investors. Not in Stage One, anyway, when they were absorbed in their work. Once they became wealthy, then—and only then—they proceeded to Stage Two, and became investors. At that point, they really had no choice.

In essence, in Stage One those who eventually became rich invested in themselves. In Stage Two, they finally had more money than could be used for that purpose, and hence turned to more traditional areas of investment.

CHAPTER FOUR

Employees—
You Don't Have to Be Self-employed
to Become Rich

The examples cited in the previous chapter may have given you the impression that the only people who became rich were High Rollers who were self-employed. They weren't the only ones, but there are indeed particular barriers to becoming wealthy which have to be hurdled by people who are employees.

Let's see what the obstacles are and how they were successfully overcome.

"THIS IS FOR ME"

We will confine our attention for the moment to people who are employed by corporations or the federal, state, or city government. How do you think such people answered the following questions?

"Financially speaking, what are you hoping to have happen

to you in your present job? What ideally would you like to see occur?"

The answer the overwhelming majority—83 percent—of the employees we surveyed gave was this: "I hope to some-how make enough money to one day do what I really want," and, "Ideally, either through my current job or some outside source, I'd like to have enough money to quit and then get on with the things that really matter to me."

The responses seem natural enough, but as you may already have guessed, they are a recipe for trouble. What it boils down to is that most employees fervently hope to proceed to Stage Two (that is, be successful investors), and then go on to Stage One, and finally do the things they find deeply absorb-ing.

The result is simple. The mass of gamblers, the really frenzied speculators of the world, aren't roaming the streets wild-eyed, muttering to themselves. They are sitting in offices all over the U.S., well dressed and to all appearances rather calm. Their actions, however, speak far more loudly than their looks.

"All I want to do is become rich," protested Steve, "and then get the hell out of here." At thirty-nine, he has been try-ing to do precisely that now for seventeen years. And how has he tried?

A typical day for Steve involves four to six calls to his stockbroker. Commodities, stocks, and particularly stock op-tions occupy a fair amount of his time and attention. He is convinced that sooner or later he is "going to hit it big," as he puts it. "The leverage is tremendous. All I need is one good one."

Although he has been at it since 1971, he has yet to break even. "I'm still paying my dues," he said bravely. "This is a rough game." Forgetting what it has cost him in money, it is interesting to see what portion of each day is being consumed by his investment activities.

Steve's workday averages six and a half hours (eight, minus one and a half for lunch). Approximately one hour and twenty minutes of the six and a half are devoted to the market, in one way or another. Either Steve is reading yesterday's prices in the morning paper or reports he receives from his broker and from an expensive investment advisory service he subscribes to, or else he is on the phone with his broker or with one of three friends who also play the market, with whom he constantly compares notes.

In spite of that, he does manage to get his work done each day. It's not his employer who is being cheated. It is Steve. For even aside from the money he loses (an average of $1,300 per year), what we need to ask is: Could the time and attention be used for more productive purposes? Steve's repeatedly stated goal, after all, has been "to free myself to do what I want to do."

When he is asked, "Why can't you do what you want to do now?" he always has his answer ready. "Money," he states flatly, "I don't have the money."

The millions of men and women who are in Steve's position can't all be wrong when they say that a lack of money is what is stopping them. Yet, there has to be more to the story. Something of profound importance has clearly been omitted, for like Steve, most have gone through a lot of money which could have been used to pursue the things they enjoy doing.

Stripped to its essentials, the fundamental difference between being an employee and being self-employed is this: very few employees are able to make accidental investing an integral part of their workday.

You might be amused to know that the most money-hungry people we began studying two decades ago all either wanted to—or did—work in real estate or stockbrokers' offices. Unconsciously, they reasoned that, if they worked all day around buildings or securities, they would automatically be able to take their paychecks and invest them in the very objects they handled each day.

Everything was going to get deliciously mixed up: first, they'd make money by buying or selling a building or stock for a customer, and with the commission money they'd receive, they planned to buy a building or stock for themselves, which they'd either keep or else sell to the next customer, for a substantial profit. Their workday and their investing activities were going to easily and naturally be combined.

In sum, Stage One and Stage Two would exist side by side: they were going to enjoy playing with stocks and real estate for a living *and* they would inevitably wind up owning some for themselves.

Rarely did it work out that way, as we'll later see. But their picture—false though it turned out to be—tells us why employees usually find it so hard to become rich. That exciting mixture of enjoyable work and profitable investing is simply not available to them. For most, job-related activities are quite separate from any investing they also choose to do. In fact, as was the case with Steve, the two areas compete for time and attention. So, like Steve, most employees favor one over the other. "And why shouldn't I?" Steve asked. "One of them is for *me*."

RICH, BY STAGES

Steve's comment says it all. In studying who becomes rich, and why, two distinct stages emerged. In Stage One, those who ultimately became rich were profoundly absorbed by a particular activity. Thanks to the fact that they were so caught up in it, they accidentally persisted in doing it, and hence eventually excelled at it. Then, in Stage Two, they became investors, because the activity they excelled at produced more income than they could invest in themselves.

Key question: Which of the two stages meant more to the people who became millionaires? None had to even think about the answer. It was Stage One. "After I sold my business," said one, age forty, "I was lost." But you had all that money ($3.4 million, in this instance). "So what?" he said. "It wasn't the same."

Yet, amazingly, which of the two stages does Steve feel is

the more personally meaningful to him? Which stage does he, and millions like him, identify as being "for *me*"? Stage Two, his investment activities.

What characterized developing millionaires is that they unintentionally proceeded from Stage One to Stage Two. What characterized people who failed was that they intentionally tried—repeatedly—to go from Stage Two to Stage One. Few ever made it out of Stage Two. Are you surprised that they were—and still are—so frustrated, anxious, and annoyed?

Steve's problem isn't merely personal; it's also institutional. How do you go about investing in a business that's not yours? If it is publicly owned, you can buy some stock. But more than half the employees we studied either worked for companies which were not publicly owned or else the Government. And as one, a mailman, said, "I wouldn't buy shares in the post office even if they *were* selling them."

Assuming for the moment that the company you work for is publicly owned, and you do decide to buy some of its shares, what would you do with the stock you'd bought if you were fired, or quit? Also, how much of your income would you spend on the company's stock, if you decided to buy any at all? And finally, once you start investing in the stock, will you notice it?

Wendy never did. And that, more than anything else, is what allowed her to be so patient and let her investment grow. Wendy's and Steve's positions thus stand in stark contrast to one another. The company for which he works is public and its shares are traded on the New York Stock Exchange, yet any money he chose to invest in its stock would be drawn from his after-tax income, whereas those who are self-employed are investing pre-tax dollars. That's two dollars for the price of one, in this case. More importantly, however, Steve can't help being aware of every dollar he decides to spend on his company's stock. And that is a major complication, since those who invest consciously are inevitably impatient.

As long as they are looking for profit, they will ultimately seek to maximize that profit. That indeed is what Steve tries to do. "Why don't you invest in your company's stock purchase program?" he was asked. "Because," he replied confidently, "I can do better on my own, in the market." Steve's company is a multibillion-dollar outfit, and its slow-moving stock isn't one he finds it worthwhile to play. Investors like him, not employed by his firm, feel much the same way. Smaller, speculative issues appeal more to Steve. "With them," he says, "I might just get lucky."

In spite of years of trying, it hasn't yet happened. But he has determination and intends to keep looking. Since his investing is conscious, and hence too restless, our results indicate the odds are high that he'll not find what he's looking for.

Who will, then? Which employees became wealthy, and how did they do it?

Let's look at one well-known figure who has clearly succeeded. When we asked Harding Lawrence, the Chairman and Chief Executive Officer of Braniff, what it takes, he responded bluntly, "Don't set compensation as a goal. Find work you like, and the compensation will follow."

"As simple as that?" we inquired. "No," he replied. "You'll probably have to ask for it sooner or later, otherwise you might not get the pay you want. Your firm isn't going to just hand it to you. But if money is a large part of your thinking, you won't do really good work, and that's what matters most. That, in the end, is why you'll be paid well. It won't—it can't —come to you just because you want it to. You have to subordinate yourself to a larger goal.

"I didn't start out in life to become rich," he said quietly. "I set out to be involved in the business which was the most interesting to me—air transportation. I wouldn't have been happy in any other field, no matter how much I earned there. To me, there was no alternative, no second choice. *This* was the field I loved. It wasn't a vocation. It was an avocation. I couldn't wait to get to work in the morning.

"By the way, that doesn't mean there weren't plenty of

problems to face. There were. Every day. When you least expect it, you can count on a major crisis to suddenly appear. But no matter how many setbacks you experience, you can't let it slow you down to the point where it takes you out of the game."

Lawrence has stayed with it, through the good years and the bad, and in 1978 was the sixth most highly paid corporate executive in the United States, earning $1,940,636. When we asked him whether young people who eventually want to become rich should go into business on their own, he replied firmly, "Absolutely not. They're wrong to think that that's the only way they'll ever become millionaires."

UNWITTINGLY WEALTHY

Let's examine a few representative cases from our sample, and see precisely why they became wealthy.

In high school and college, Harvey was an introverted youngster who loved music. Shy to the point of seeming asocial at times, he found himself drawn to the piano, which he practiced three to four hours a day. He did some composing, as well. "Rodgers and Hammerstein stuff," he labeled it. Occasionally, he dreamed of being a concert pianist, but was aware that although he played well, others played better. Nor, he knew, was he about to devote the time and energy needed to catch up, much less surpass them.

A history major in college ("studying music would have taken the fun out of it," he commented), his first few jobs were throwaways. In one, Harvey was the record reviewer and entertainment columnist ("What's Happening Where") for a small-town newspaper. His desire to be around music finally led him to take a job with a record company, a position which allowed a variety of his skills to develop.

He wasn't a professional composer, but he didn't have to be, either. Of far more interest to his supervisors was that Harvey be able to recognize when someone had a potential hit. There were composers, writers, singers, and musicians everywhere. Instead of needing more of them, the company had to find a way of selecting which ones to spend its money on. Harvey viewed the position as a terribly dictatorial one, and even after fourteen years in the business, working under a succession of bosses who came and went, he still wasn't ready to be the one who'd point the finger, and say, "You, stay. And you, you can go."

Quietly, in the background, Harvey made the crucial judgments about what would and would not sell, decisions his bosses then proudly announced as their own. They basked endlessly in the spotlight he so diligently avoided. Actually, it was a happy marriage; it would not have even occurred to him to ask for a piece of the stage. As an invaluable part of the business, however, he periodically received substantial increases in pay.

And how did Harvey, a Low Roller, finally make his million? One of his two bosses decided to resign in order to form a company of his own. Taking Harvey and some of the best sales people with him, the new company soon prospered. In lieu of the high salary he had been receiving, Harvey received a moderate salary and 33⅓ percent of the stock of the fledgling outfit. Three years later, with business booming, the company was acquired by a well-known conglomerate for more than $4 million.

Ralph exemplifies a different route. A tall, ungainly youngster who had little interest in sports, he was able to make his actions seem more fluid and in control mainly by slowing them down. His words and behavior are now habitually cautious and measured, so much so Ralph should be free of the fear that he'll make a fool of himself. He should be, but he's not. In fact, although he seems to be a certified No Roller, agonizing publicly about every cent he spends, he is actually a High Roller afraid to come stumbling out of the closet. The rigid grip he has on his behavior prevents any spontaneity from emerging.

His mind, though, isn't similarly suppressed, and over the

years he has had some first-rate ideas. For eleven years, from 1963 to 1974, he worked for a mid-sized supplier of specialty chemicals. During December of the final year, one of the workers in the warehouse fell, dropping a case he was holding which contained four gallon-jars of a strong acid. The case and two of the jars shattered, covering the worker's arms, neck, and face. Quick action on the part of a co-worker prevented blindness, though extensive scarring resulted.

Ralph, who at the time was a product manager, resolved that there would be no recurrences. Within three months, he was able to convince top management to let him design a safer line of containers for the company's products, which they themselves would then proceed to manufacture.

The joy of designing, constructing, and then destroying the prototype containers, in order to test their bursting strength, was more than even *he* could hide. Ralph had long been interested in the packaging business, had come to know a great deal about the field, and was currently responsible for selecting the materials used for storing and shipping the company's products.

Now he was free to produce his own. When management saw the price tag for setting up a new manufacturing facility, they balked. Business in 1974 and particularly in early '75 was not good, and they were ready to scrap the project. Ralph, in what at the time he called "an act of faith" and we'd call the High Roller in Ralph coming to the surface, offered to go 50-50. He would put up half the money and own half the stock; they'd provide the other half. His $72,000 annual salary was to be more than halved, to $30,000. They agreed.

At first, the company bought all the packaging and storage systems Ralph's outfit could produce. Soon, however, he was selling to other companies, as well, and within four years Ralph's little outfit was no longer so little. Finally, in February of 1979, the parent company, its sales and profits having grown considerably, and its cash position good, offered to buy Ralph's 50 percent. He had invested $130,000 in cash of his own money, and he was to get back five times the average earnings of the packaging concern over the next three years, an amount which promises to bring him in the neighborhood of $1.1 to $1.3 million. He has already received $850,000, on account.

Ellen, our next instance, isn't what she seems to be. Given to saying aloud almost anything that is on her mind, she strikes many as scatterbrained. She is anything but. Our thoughts usually change almost as often as the topics of her sentences do, but if we are talking about something we normally continue on with the subject, in spite of other thoughts which may cross our mind. She doesn't. In her case, thought and speech seem too closely connected.

Her interest in designing apparel was present early, and strongly. After graduating from a fashion institute, she got a job as an assistant designer. A year later she moved to another firm, and two years after that, to a third. Almost without exception, people initially mistake her uninhibited comments as an indication that she must be a High Roller. She isn't. In fact, appearances aside, she is one of the more tightfisted people we studied, careful with every cent and inclined to agonize privately about anything she considers financial foolishness on her own part.

That cost-control inclination served her well in her third job, where she became a valued associate to a well-known designer. Talented and extremely hard-working, her efforts were increasingly well rewarded. Over a twelve-year span, her salary made its way to almost $50,000 a year. A few years later, her famous boss died, and Ellen's plans seemed in disarray. But a decision by the firm's owners to continue operating turned what had appeared to be a tragedy into a boon for Ellen. She was apparently the only one who knew every aspect of the firm's operations and who could readily "design in the same style" as her boss previously had. A pay package was put together guaranteeing her in excess of $160,000 a year. Living simply, but nicely, she has indeed saved her way to a net worth of more than $1 million.

MONEYED MANAGERS

We followed a number of others who wound up holding key executive positions similar to Ellen's. And in certain instances, they too saved their way to a net asset value exceeding $1 million.

The expansion of the company for which they worked, rather than the death or retirement of its top people, usually created the openings they then filled. By the time they moved into the top slots, though, their annual earnings were substantial. And if they saved a decent portion of what they earned, it wasn't difficult for them to eventually become reasonably wealthy.

That, more than anything else, is what excited Henry when he thought about being Vice-President of his firm. He didn't intend to put his $150,000 a year salary in the bank. His mind continually envisioned all the wonderful things he could buy, if only he had a salary that large. For the moment, however, he was earning a mere $38,000.

What needs to be emphasized here is that some who wanted to be rich went directly after money. Others, however, went after it indirectly, and wanted to be managers.

They viewed top management positions as being much like a faucet, and no matter how much money was needed, and how often, it would always be there. "Those people don't have *any* money worries," Henry told us, "and I'm not going to, either." "Will you save some portion of your $3,000 a week paycheck, once you are receiving it?" we asked. "Just let me get my hands on it first," he replied immediately, "then, I'll see."

You already know what happened to employees who attempted to go from Stage Two to Stage One—that is, to become rich *before* they found activities they deeply enjoyed doing. Well then, how about those who wanted to be highly paid executives? If in their mind "top management" meant "top dollar," did they get there more quickly, more slowly, or not at all? What's your guess?

By now you probably won't be surprised to discover that the answer usually was, "Not at all."

But why? What stopped them? Shouldn't all the money they correctly saw sitting at the end of the road have motivated them to cover the distance to it more rapidly? It should indeed have, and when the study first began we assumed it would help them get there. And quickly, at that.

But it didn't. Quite the contrary; those who wanted money most, and thought a top management position would get them an abundance of it, rarely wound up becoming highly paid.

Henry's case is typical. He looked at the lavish life-style many executives enjoyed and he knew without a doubt what he'd have to do. He too would have to become an executive. "Maybe something besides money motivated them?" he was asked. "Oh yeah?" he replied. "You mean it's only an accident that they live in mansions and have Cadillacs and Mercedes in the driveway?"

He did have a point. After all, if they weren't interested in money, how come they wound up with so much of it?

As it turned out, they did indeed have to have an interest in money. But what our results clearly show is that if that interest was too strong, it interfered substantially with their efforts to become wealthy. And for a very good reason: they were too impatient. Sound familiar? It is, and we need to see why great impatience proved so great an impediment to promotion.

In the office next door to Henry's sat Frank. What makes these two interesting is that they are alike in many ways, yet only one of the two was to be chosen to fill a slot vacated by a superior of theirs, who had been moved up a notch. Three people were to make the decision, jointly. Although each of the three had some idea of what Henry and Frank were like, it was an important position and a formal review was conducted to decide who'd be given it.

In a meeting with the three, Henry was asked about his interest in, experience at, and qualifications for the position.

Near the end of the interview, Henry stated bluntly what he had frequently said in one form or another: "I'm the man for the job."

Although none of the three said anything at the time, either to Henry or to one another, they were enormously offended by the comment. They didn't want him to say that to *them;* they wanted to be the ones saying that to *him.*

It was normal practice for Henry to pat himself publicly on the back. Those who heard him labeled him an egotist and a narcissist. Actually, he was neither. He was in a hurry.

One of the best ways to sell such things as houses, clothes, and cars is to use the following powerful sales pitch: "If you want to get there, act as if you are already there." According to the pitch, you should live in the right location, dress in the right clothes, drink the right liquor, and drive the right car, since people will think you've already made it—and hence you *will* make it. Needless to say, what's "right" in each of these instances is whatever the advertiser is trying to sell you at the time. Almost without exception, there was only one place such products could help you get: deeper in debt. Be that as it may, the ad's pitch is simple but effective: If you are a convincing enough fake, it says, sooner or later you will be real.

It is so widely used a sales technique, Henry and a huge number of others use it to sell themselves. He wants so desperately to be there, he tries to act as if he already is. When he publicly sings his own praises, he is merely attempting to convince you (this time, with words) that he is all the things he says he is. Like the many others who've swallowed the message of the ad, and who are acting accordingly, he is a fake, trying to become real. In short, self-congratulatory comments are a tool impatiently ambitious people unwittingly use to try to sell themselves to you.

Are you buying? Henry's bosses didn't, and yours probably won't either. This is not a book on business etiquette, and if you feel you should act in a particular way, don't let anything you read here stop you. But consider the evidence. Over a twenty-year period we have asked just over 400 people who were in a significant hiring-and-firing position, or who had the power to promote or demote, whether they usually believed a self-flattering remark made by a subordinate, and if they did, did such comments act to speed the person's promotion.

Not only did a self-congratulatory comment make 91 percent of the 400 suspicious, it brought forth a certain belligerence, a you-better-be-able-to-prove-it attitude. That made any blunders the employee subsequently made, which might have gone unnoticed otherwise, stand out like a sore thumb.

Quite apart from anything Henry said, there was the matter of what he did. Namely, nothing. His intense desire to be a wealthy executive made him scornful of small details of any sort. "Why should I have to deal with this sort of crap?" he asked exasperatedly. Unfortunately, petty details are an essential and abundant part of every aspect of business.

Their existence therefore isn't the real issue. Your response to them is. You can make a mountain out of any molehill, if you want to. And what we discovered is that someone is likely to do precisely that if they don't happen to like their job. In fact, the more they dislike it, the more resentful they are likely to be about its petty details. To put it more positively: people who enjoyed their work usually didn't notice the many details connected with each task they had to attend to.

Rita and Pam provide an instance of what typically occurred. Both began working for a large printing firm at about the same time. Within a few years, it was apparent that although the two encountered the same dose of daily difficulties, they reacted very differently to them. Rita quietly completed a host of tasks which Pam found irritating. What was revealing was that Rita often felt sorry for the problems Pam was having. What made her expression of sympathy so remarkable was that she herself was performing the very same duties, and did so with nary a peep. Nor was she being a martyr, suffering silently. The many details which annoyed Pam Rita didn't even notice.

It gave Rita enormous satisfaction to do her job well. In a business in which even minor errors may look major to customers, Rita enjoyed seeing quality work produced. "We don't always do it flawlessly," she said, but she was indeed prepared to try. More importantly, she was visibly pleased when the work she did had what she called, "the look of perfection."

Pam, too, tried. Both were skilled, and in time moved up. Yet, an incident four years later finally brought all the underlying factors to the surface. A regular customer, the owner of a number of restaurants, dropped off some work to be done. He returned a while later, just as Pam had finished having the machine set up to do the work. He had decided to use a heavier weight paper. Pam was annoyed, and mutely allowed the message to be conveyed. Without saying anything to the customer, too irritated to even look at him, she changed the required work order.

It wasn't the first time he changed the grade of paper he had used for the work he was having done, but it was his first contact with Pam. Usually Rita, or someone else, processed his order. He found the contrast in attitude strikingly unwelcome. He particularly didn't appreciate hearing her say to her co-workers as she walked away, "Why can't people just make up their minds?"

When we later asked Rita why she too didn't object to having to switch paper, perhaps right in the middle of a job, her reply was, "It's not a big deal. It only takes a few seconds." Her next comment was especially telling: "Besides, it's interesting to see how it looks on different kinds of paper."

The restaurant owner casually mentioned the incident to the woman who owned the printing firm, who made a mental note of it. "It upset me," she said. "He's a good customer. He's no complainer." Without mentioning the episode to Pam, she watched. And the differences between Pam and Rita suddenly became clearer than ever to her. With business expanding, she needed a manager, and two months later it was Rita who was offered the job, at more than twice her previous pay.

No one example we look at can be conclusive. Individual factors, unique to that instance, could account for the outcome. Yet when hundreds of cases are examined, pairs of people who were approximately equal in ability and energy but who did not do equally well, certain conclusions become inescapable. Here the connection was strong enough to be predictive: those who found the minor details of their work a major annoyance did not persist, and became wealthy significantly less often. They complained more, but in fact, they did less, and as the years went by, their earnings showed it.

Indeed, the Ritas and Franks we studied outdistanced the Pams and Henrys by a considerable distance. We were told repeatedly by a number of employees, anxious to get to the top, that if you don't make any noise no one notices you. That turned out not to be so. Workers who were good, and whose continuing interest in their work nearly guaranteed that they'd get better, were very definitely not overlooked. There may not have been a party thrown for them every time they casually displayed their competence, but it did register, and was remembered. Somehow, people notice.

CHAPTER FIVE

Luck—
What Is It
and Who Has It?

Pam and Henry are convinced they'll not get the recognition they deserve. So they lobby, loudly, wanting to be sure to catch your eye. Not only are they both in a hurry, they want to be associated only with great and glorious achievements. A petty project scares them: they want people to think of them in grand and glowing terms, not as someone who does "menial stuff," as Pam calls it, "the kinds of things *anyone* could do." Their most important goal, one they pursue unconsciously but intensely, is persuading you of their superiority and importance. Often they overdo it, to the point of being, at worst, offensive, and at best, overbearing.

It would be a mistake, though, to be too critical of them. There is, after all, a bit of Pam and Henry in each of us. We all want to do great things and be rewarded for our efforts by the arrival of fame and fortune no later than 9 A.M. tomorrow morning, please. It's almost too easy to talk about something instead of doing it—until it's too late to do it at all. And once we've fallen behind, lobbying becomes even more necessary. No one wants to be considered inadequate, or inferior.

Interestingly enough, it was frequently the quietest people in our sample, who went on to become the wealthiest. They weren't quietest in the sense that they spoke in a whisper. Volume had nothing to do with it. Some spoke loudly, others softly. But they said very little about their work. In fact, they were conspicuously reluctant to discuss it at length, almost as if they'd lose their grip on it if they did. They were sufficiently involved with it so that stepping back and talking easily and endlessly about it was nearly impossible.

Sam, for instance, is a sociable sort. Easygoing and down to earth, he majored in English in college and after graduation got a job with a publishing firm. For eighteen years, he rose steadily through the ranks, switching firms three times in the process. A four-year stint in marketing later proved advantageous, but it was the editorial end of the publishing business that most intrigued him.

Without intending it to happen, over the years he had become well known as an editor of self-help books. "I've become type-cast," he chuckled, "much the way actors are." The characterization had resulted from his being the one responsible for the shaping of two quite successful self-help titles, each of which had sold hundreds of thousands of copies. Although he bridled somewhat when first saddled with the label, commenting defensively, "I *do* do other kinds of books, you know," he soon forgot about it.

In his view, it was something of an accident that he had been so labeled in the first place. But what happened next was certainly no accident. As he put it, "I realized, 'If they can do it, so can I.'" He considered both books superficial, and "I knew mine would at least be no worse." In the first frankly commercial project he had ever undertaken, he threw a book together in less than three months—"bits and pieces," he called them, "anything I could think of." In time-honored fashion, he got another publisher, rather than his own firm, to do the book. It did surprisingly well, and two more followed. He has made over $800,000, thus far.

Vic and Linda's experience was similar, though in computers, not publishing. He had learned computer programming as an undergraduate and then graduate student in electrical engineering. Linda's knowledge of the field was the result of four and a half years with IBM.

They met at work, and became inseparable, often consulting with one another on the workaday problems they were given to solve. Their friends joked that it was difficult to tell if they were a romantic or business couple. The distinction became even more difficult to make, as the two soon got married and in essence went into business together. Like Sam, they were No Rollers, and they too wanted to remain part of a large corporate entity.

It took time, but within five months they were able to convince the owners of the firm to allow them (and a friend of theirs) to start a new subsidiary, which would supply software services to other firms. At one point during the negotiations, the three threatened to leave. They didn't mean it, but exasperated at the lack of progress, said it anyway. It worked. They were given the "piece of the action" they had asked for: 10 percent of the stock of the new enterprise to begin with, and 10 percent more each year until, after four years, they would own half the business. Linda's comment, made during the second year their company was operating, is revealing: "We were managing to handle their software needs, and they're a real pain in the neck. Everyone else's problems just *had* to be easier."

The increasing number of small computers being sold to businesses of modest size gave Vic and Linda the opportunity they needed. Since they were living in a part of the U.S. which does not have the same excess of competition in this field that larger, urban centers do, they were able to carve out a nice position for themselves.

Vic and Linda fought a lot. Spending morning, noon, and night together, and having such contrasting ways of doing things, some conflict was probably inevitable. But their business grew very rapidly in the subsequent nine years, and they were recently offered $1.35 million for their share of it by one of the giants in the industry. They have instead decided to buy the 50 percent they do not now own and continue operating as they've been.

We could provide many other examples of people who did remarkably well but along the way said little about it. Indeed, Rita, Frank, Sam, Vic, and Linda, all together, don't say enough in a week to match the quantity of complaining Pam and Henry do each day. What is truly amazing, however, is the number of times quietly successful people have been accused of being lucky.

What a strange accusation that is. Is it luck that allowed Sam, Linda, and Vic to plug themselves into a system whose operation they had come to know so well, one which had been used to help others and was now going to be used to help those who had been running it? One hostile critic saw it differently: "They were simply there at the right time."

They were indeed. But they had been there at the wrong time, too: eighteen years in Sam's case, fifteen in Vic's, and seventeen in Linda's. The key question has to be: What kept them going all those years? The thought, "One day I'm going to get lucky," would not have done it. We've studied the reactions of hundreds of people who have spent years feverishly hoping to "get lucky," and unfortunately for them, two things usually happened instead.

First, the petty details, the minor aspects of their work became so annoying, they simply weren't done. It was fascinating to watch what happened when someone tried to concentrate only on the more majestic parts of their work and not bother with the what they felt were the more undignified parts. The little rivets which hold huge beams in place can probably be omitted in large numbers in the basement and not be missed. But as construction work proceeds, and the building grows taller, the higher floors press with increasing weight on the lower. Then if the wind starts blowing . . .

Many had avoided for years what they considered the trivial details of their work—and then one day were shocked to discover how shoddy their efforts had been all along. At that point, they finally became both furious and fed up. "Who needs all this bullshit?" one demanded. "All it *is* is a mass of details." That is indeed what it had become. The many seemingly minor items had at last accumulated to form a pile too high to be ignored any longer. Defeated (but on the surface, angry), they quit.

OBNOXIOUSLY PETTY PEOPLE

We don't mean to glorify trivia in saying that a mass of missed details can bring a sizable structure down. There are plenty of people who thrive on pettiness. They want you to think their minuscule area of activity is absolutely crucial to the world's being intact tomorrow.

"Everyone always *wants* something from me," said Harold, who teaches applied mathematics at an Ivy League university, "and I have to have my teeth fixed again." In a survey of Harold's colleagues, ten of twelve voted him the least productive, most useless person in the department, a man who spends all his time hiding. His constant nit-picking has earned him the contempt of his students and the nickname, "Professor Fuss 'n' Quibble." Tenure and his grip on "committee work" have allowed him to keep his job.

Caroline works as an assistant editor at a nationally known magazine. Recently she received an important note from a staff reporter correcting an item in a story of his they were about to run. "I will not read notes like these," she told the reporter on the phone, "unless the words are more evenly spaced. There should be the same distance between each word and the next. Do you understand?" Much to the reporter's distress, she hadn't even read the note. The magazine later had to print a retraction.

Harold and Caroline are devoting their lives to making

mountains of every last molehill they find in their tiny backyard. They have a pail of rusting rivets, but no intention of using them to build anything. Let us hope that people like these two don't manage to seriously interfere with your attempts to accomplish something.

SMALL STEPS, MAJOR CONSEQUENCES

Neither focusing solely on the details nor ignoring them altogether is wise. Something in between is obviously called for. And strangely enough, the people who accidentally located that Golden Mean were those who profoundly enjoyed doing their work. Their absorption in it also allowed time to pass far more quickly than it did for others doing the same work, but who found it irritating.

Somewhere down the road, with time quickly passing by, luck did indeed play a role. Whether they'd happily been at it for ten, twenty, or even thirty years, they suddenly saw an interesting opportunity. Although intriguing, it didn't strike them as anything extraordinary. Few were aware of the momentous consequences their actions would have. In fact, they were usually among the last to realize they had just taken a step which would make them a millionaire.

Art Rooney is the owner of the Pittsburgh Steelers. He told us, "You just can't plan for some of the best things that ever happen to you. Joe Carr, who was the first Commissioner of the National Football League, asked me in the late 1920s to get a team together. My sandlot teams were very good, and he wanted me to enter one in the NFL.

"There were too many problems, though. College football was the big thing at the time. That ruled out games on Saturday, when everyone was watching the colleges play. Sunday was out, too, because there were Blue Laws in effect then in Pennsylvania. Strong ones. You couldn't do anything on Sunday. But I loved playing ball, and managing teams, and just kept on doing it.

"In 1933, when the Depression was severe, they lifted the Blue Laws in Pennsylvania. I didn't think they ever would. It was then that I bought an NFL franchise. I figured at least we'd finally be able to play ball. I paid $2,500 for it."

It's worth over $25 million now. We have recently talked to the heads of two major corporations who want to buy Rooney's franchise. "I'd start at $25 million," said one, "and pay more. But he won't sell. He has five sons. They'll wind up with the business."

Nina Blanchard's experiences were similar. She is the owner and director of the West Coast's leading modeling and talent agency, but arrived at that position only after a series of jobs —and mishaps—which made the last, successful step seem largely a matter of luck. As we'll see, it was anything but.

She told us, "I started out in the 1950s doing makeup at NBC." Her skill developed rapidly, and by 1957 she was the highest paid makeup artist in New York. "Somehow, I *knew* about faces," she said. "Only later did I also discover that I had knowledge I didn't know I had."

Two problems arose. "I'd done all kinds of things, and done them well. What I couldn't do was keep a job. I couldn't have a boss. As soon as someone started telling me what to do, it was over." The only course open to her, she concluded, was to be in business for herself.

The second problem was her honesty: "As far as I'm concerned, lying to someone is the worst thing you can do to them. Usually, it's just cruel. Misleading them hurts them much more than telling them the truth ever would."

That policy, however, nearly guaranteed she'd not do well when she opened a muffler shop in Arizona (where she went looking for some "peace and quiet"), and then a charm school in Los Angeles. Thanks to her success at NBC, she had some money. As she put it, "I had saved enough to be able to *lose* $87,000 in the muffler business." Her competitors even told her what to do to turn a decent profit, but she hadn't done it. "You can't *tell*'em," they'd said. "You have to *sell*'em." Later, the charm school too went under, and she went bankrupt. "I couldn't promise my students our courses would make their dreams come true. So they left, and enrolled with people who *would* make those promises."

In 1961, she started a modeling agency and became totally immersed in what she was doing. Everything she had learned in the past now became useful. "I used to *drive* my first important model to the jobs I had just booked for her at an account I had just gotten as a result of a brochure I had just prepared. Then—and now—many of my clients even stayed in my home when they're working."

There were some hard times along the way, but as she put it, "We cut back, and survived. I had been rich, poor, and everything in between, both as a kid and as an adult, and that made it a lot easier to get through the dry spells."

Finally, when she became well established, offers to buy her firm came in regularly. As involved as ever, she continues to do well, and has no intention of selling.

A FORTUNE WITHOUT FANFARE

Put simply, almost none of the people we studied became rich doing the thing they started out to do. No matter how many years they had been occupied by one activity, something else —sometimes very different, usually only moderately so— generated the bulk of their fortune. And rather rapidly, at that.

That was so unexpected a finding, one which took us completely by surprise, it is worth looking at carefully.

The fact that Wendy's wealth came to her through the sale of the building which housed her business, rather than the business itself, at first appeared to be an isolated instance. When all the cases were taken together, however, what at first seemed an isolated phenomenon was seen to recur with great regularity. In fact, although we are speaking here of a diverse collection of people, with little in common, the one feature they did have was this: almost all appear to have stumbled their way into being rich. Moreover, it occurred during a relatively short time span of very high income, following a much longer span of far more moderate earnings.

Was that merely luck? A stroke of fortune? If so, it could —and should—have happened to others, as well. Of the 1,057 people we studied, the 83 who became millionaires should have been randomly distributed throughout. And that, they certainly were not.

What characterized the 83, and set them worlds apart from the rest, was the degree to which year in and year out they were absorbed by their work. Long before they knew whether they'd be paid enough to support themselves, much less become wealthy, they were caught up in their work and doing far more of it than they realized. Even the petty stuff: they did that, too. Not that they liked it. Almost no one does, but they did it anyway, and barely even noticed it.

And then, somewhere down the road, typically after a waiting period of almost two decades, luck did indeed find them. But—and a very big but it is—precisely because they did not see it as their "chance of a lifetime," the "one—and only one —opportunity" they'd ever have, they did not leap crazily at it. They walked, not ran, toward it. Amazingly, it lacked the do-or-die character it would have had for someone less caught up in their work.

The absence of panic-and-plunge behavior was conspicuous, particularly because we studied so many people who react no other way, and who appear to be spending their entire lives in a dither, waiting nervously for fortune to find them. On the other hand, those who were to become millionaires took the fateful step without fanfare. They viewed what they were doing from a different angle. "It is," said one, "just an extension of what I'm doing now." Consequently, there was little to think about, especially since few realized the size of the financial rewards their new undertaking would bring them.

PUBLICLY ACCEPTABLE ANSWERS

What is almost amusing is the large number of millionaires—
68 of 83, almost 82 percent—who themselves attributed their
success to luck. Are they wrong? They are indeed. They
don't want you to think they are bragging. "The whole thing
just fell in my lap," said one. "The offer was made," said another, "and I thought, 'Why not?'" "It really wasn't any of
my doing," said a third. Those sentences, as opposed to, "Yes,
I'm wonderful, and *that* is the reason I became rich," are
much more palatable, and hence they'll keep coming.

Some, though, attributed their growing wealth to a friend,
mentor, or their parents, instead of (or in addition to) luck. "I
could feel my late father's guiding hand. He taught me a lot,"
said one. "I owe it all to my mother," said another. Perhaps.
But Mom and Dad had other children, too—the 83 millionaires had 256 brothers and sisters—who thus far at least show
no sign of being set to do anything comparable on their own.

About 43 percent (36 of 83) also attributed their becoming
wealthy to a strong interest in money. Over the years, one of
the responses they gave to questions such as, "What makes
you work so hard?" and, "What prompts you to put in such
long hours?" was "Oh, the money, of course."

Sounds reasonable, doesn't it? Almost too much so. This
one is tricky, because while money did indeed provide part of
their motivation, it was a much smaller part than they would
have you believe. First of all, many were doing things which
didn't pay them very well and which they had good reason to
believe never would.

Secondly, with a minor shift in the nature of their work,
they could have made substantially more money than they
were making. But they were unwilling to even entertain the
thought. One had said, "No, I'm not interested in making any
changes; I want to get paid big bucks for doing it *this way*."

Is this person more concerned with money or with what he enjoys doing?

Finally, and more significantly, it was illuminating to see what happened when they had more money than they could spend. "It's habit, I guess, that keeps me going," said one. "I've become a workaholic, you know," said another, "otherwise I'd stop."

Don't you believe it. The woman who made the latter comment loves her work, and if she hadn't, she'd not have remained immersed totally in it for so many years. Now she's worth over $1.15 million, lives quite plainly—and works, harder than ever. Even having a billion dollars wouldn't slow her down, because money wasn't the prime mover to begin with.

In a society that values wealth as much as ours does, it is hardly surprising that people who have a great deal of money feel themselves to be somewhat abnormal, and thus often bend over backward to present themselves as being "just like you and me."

When all is said and done, most people don't know why they work as hard as they do. The massive amounts of time they allow their work to consume does require an explanation. But they are hoping no one asks for it. Those who do will, of course, be given something "acceptable."

Standards of acceptability change, however. During periods of high inflation, for example, there was a significant increase in the number of people who told us that money was what made them work with such intensity. Everyone was having trouble keeping up, and at such times it is apparently all right to tell people your motivations are financial.

Nevertheless, whether the rate of inflation was high or low, those who eventually became millionaires stayed highly involved with their work. If we take them at their word, we'll have to conclude that whenever the rate of inflation decreased, they somehow managed to conveniently fish up the needed supplementary motivation elsewhere.

Well, if it wasn't luck, Mom and Dad, or money that was

responsible—although each of these factors is undeniably important—what was? Whether they like it or not (and they certainly don't), it is they themselves who will have to take the credit. They persisted because they didn't realize that that is what they were doing, and hence made their own luck.

CHAPTER SIX

Mellowing—
Why Growing Older
Made It Easier
to Become Rich

"If you don't make it when you're young," said Ricky, "you won't make it later, either." And for that reason, he has been pushing himself harder with each passing year.

Is he right? We know that, generally speaking, people do become wealthier as they grow older. But Ricky has something more dramatic in mind than a gradual increase. As he put it, "Who wants to start out with nothing and wind up with two times nothing?"

The real question then is this: If you haven't made your million by the time you are forty, do your chances of becoming rich start to decrease? Most of the people we studied were convinced the answer was "yes." Nevertheless, that turned out not to be the case, and it is worthwhile to see why.

Oscar Dystel, for one, considers Ricky's comment to be "silly." Although Dystel is now Chairman and Chief Executive Officer of Bantam Books, the world's largest paperback publisher, when he joined the firm twenty-six years ago, at age forty-two, he hadn't previously been in the book business. Magazines were his field. The switch represented a significant mid-career change for him. In some ways, though, he remained on familiar territory. Ever since high school, he had wanted to be in the publishing field, and in spite of the shift from magazines to paperbacks, he still was.

The experience allowed him to come to a fascinating conclusion. "I didn't want to be involved with other media," he told us. "The medium which intrigued me most was the printed word. I wasn't certain at the time, but I am now: there are always plenty of new paths open to you which allow you to still stay within the field of your choice.

"If someone were to try to duplicate now what I did then, they'd probably not be able to. Our industry has reached maturity; it's not as wide open as it used to be. Avon, Fawcett, Pocket Books, NAL, Dell, and Warner are all aggressive, and sharp, and give us solid, first-class competition *every* step of the way.

"That's usually how things work out, after a while. Someone who achieves success in an older field becomes well known, and naturally, you want to do the same. But it is hard to copy them. Since the field *is* older now, it gets much more difficult to do what they did.

"Don't try. When you look at the future—when you think about where you are going—you can use only one guide: whatever *really* interests you. Don't think about money. That's never a good personal goal. The most reliable guide, the only one which can help you find your way into a clouded and unknown future, is your own involvement.

"Someone who has money as their goal is actually wandering around blinded—they have no way to tell which direction is right, for them. They won't succeed in copying what someone else did. And on this you can bet: they won't get where they want to go, either."

Something specific helped the people in our sample who ultimately became wealthy come to a similar conclusion.

"I'M NOT GOING TO LIVE FOREVER"

We couldn't pinpoint the particular moment when it occurred, but each of the people we studied at some point became consciously aware of death. They had, of course, been cognizant of it since childhood. But it is one thing to be vaguely familiar with the concept and quite another to suddenly know that sooner or later you will be dead.

It could easily have been a vastly demoralizing thought. After all, these were ambitious people who had somehow been rudely awakened to the fact that they were running out of time. Yet, instead of depressing them, in many instances (though not Ricky's) it had a beneficial effect.

Those who had become stuck doing things in a rigid and unproductive manner rather rapidly proceeded to make the small changes required to make others take them more seriously. The needed modifications were usually minor. The effect of the changes, though, was to prove major.

Charles, for instance, spent the first eleven years of his career complaining. After completing graduate school with a degree in business, he went to work for a large financial institution. He hated it, but since, as he put it, "Nothing else appeals to me more, right now," he decided to remain. What bothered him most, he said, was the sloppiness of the work the other employees were doing. Spotting other people's shortcomings was something he could do from a distance of 100 yards, even if he'd never seen the person before. To make matters worse, he usually let his caustic remarks be overheard. On occasion, he said them directly to the person's face, pointing out what he felt were embarrassing flaws he had found in their work.

So much of his time was devoted to savagely scrutinizing his co-workers' efforts, his own work suffered in the process. That was something he had little difficulty overlooking. Yet even when it was brought to his attention, he dismissed it. "I have no respect for these clowns," he stated angrily. The obvious failings of those around him interested him much more than his own.

"Why didn't they fire him?" is a question you may be asking yourself. His co-workers asked it often. But the three people who headed the division considered his work to be of a sufficiently high quality to warrant keeping him on. They did not, however, feel he deserved much if anything in the way of a raise and regularly passed over him when they increased the salary of others. After a while, it showed. The average salary he and four others initially received when they joined the firm, was $16,000. After eleven years, he was earning $34,000; they on average were at $61,000.

People labeled him hostile and disturbed, and to some extent that was so. But he was mainly full of youthful idealism, though at thirty-six whatever youthfulness he still possessed was usually buried under a scowl that was becoming a permanent part of his face. His attitude toward his work was indeed extreme. As he put it, "It should cater to the highest possible standards." That was all well and good, but neither the people in his firm nor those to whom the firm sent his reports could make much headway through his turgid, philosophical ramblings. "There's something here," stated an executive at another firm, holding the report Charles' firm had sent him, "but I'm not sure *what*."

Nothing specific occurred in the next two and a half years to make Charles' attitude change. But it did. And thoughts of death accompanied that change. "I'm giving up," he said with an air of genuine resignation. "If they want to put out garbage, I'm not going to try stopping them anymore. I'm getting old trying."

He was mellowing. His criticism had been futile, in spite of the prodigious quantity of it he had unleashed over the years. His reports became considerably easier to read, and the economic and fiscal topics he discussed became more relevant. He clearly no longer felt compelled to make his pronouncements intentionally obscure, in order both to hide what he had to say and to make himself seem "smarter than thou" as well. He gave a variety of reasons for the change, but one recurred and it was indeed accurate: "I've stopped being such a purist."

He had also finally managed to get the horse before the cart. Until that time, he wanted first and foremost to become rich, "so that I can get on to bigger and better things." For him, it wasn't a matter of certain aspects of his job being irritatingly petty. The whole thing was. Becoming wealthy was going to at last allow him to escape.

Now his thinking had changed. The fortune he had earlier expected his job to somehow bring him was nowhere in sight. He had waited for what seemed to him an eternity, and was unwilling to wait any longer. Switching firms was a thought which occurred to him frequently, and he had held a series of conversations with other, potential employers. Yet, everything was familiar at his present firm: he knew the weaknesses of everyone with whom he worked. And that made him feel strong. At another firm, they might find his flaws before he found theirs. So, he stayed.

Settling in, he found his work more intriguing and less annoying than he previously had. He also had less trouble talking to his colleagues, both in the office and out. What he at this time called "the more aggressive socializing" he began doing, and which his co-workers viewed as a rather modest effort in that direction, produced an unexpected result. At a three-day conference being held at a major hotel and convention center, events he normally shunned, he ran into the President of a competing firm who had read his reports and liked them—and remarkable as it would have sounded to Charles' old friends, liked him personally as well. They met again the next day, and Charles was offered a job at $90,000 a year, which he promptly accepted. He has been there now for almost six years, and has done better each year than the year before.

Eileen's experiences were similar, though with an interesting twist. The oldest of three daughters, Eileen was expected from an early age to excel and be a leader. Both of her parents were physicians, and they strongly encouraged all their children to strive for recognition. The parents' position in the community, where they both practiced, was a highly visible one, and they almost inevitably found themselves discussing their children's every accomplishment with the many patients and people they encountered. Bright and energetic, Eileen achieved without effort. But the pressure upon her was intense.

During high school, college, and especially graduate school, she drove herself hard, first socially and later academically, as a sociology major. Although neither she nor her parents realized it at the time, they had made no provision for failure. Sentences such as, "Win some, lose some," were never heard. Instead, whenever a setback occurred, a blaming ritual was unwittingly performed. It had to be someone's fault, and the blame was yours only if you couldn't find someone else to dump it on.

After graduation, the few journalism courses she had taken proved more valuable than the many social science courses which constituted the core of her curriculum. Without giving the matter much thought, she found first one, and then another job in the field of public relations.

There was trouble almost immediately. Although she was energetic and hard-working, willing to put in long hours and handle a variety of assignments, she found both her coworkers and employers obnoxious. "You never hear a 'thank you' around here," she said. A third and then a fourth followed, but changing firms was clearly not producing any improvement in the situation. The conclusion she came to was straightforward enough. "It's this field," she stated. "That's the way they all are in this business."

The four positions had exhausted about nine and a half years. While a variety of things bothered her about her work during that time, one stood out. It was easily the most frequently voiced complaint she made: "Everyone in this business steals from you. They don't give you any credit, and what you have, they try and take." She thus found it necessary to remain constantly alert to such thievery: "You have to watch them all like a hawk."

To some extent, her claim did seem justified. Insightful, and more importantly, quick, she was often able to come up with new ideas and spot trends before others could. Later they would arrive at the same conclusion. But since they thought they had come up with it themselves, unaided (usually, they indeed had), Eileen was unable to lay claim to all the credit she deserved. She was not, however, inclined to let the matter rest there, and frequently found herself in tense battles with others regarding who was and who was not entitled to call an idea "their own."

It was exhausting. And worse, it distracted her, preventing a concentration on the work she was supposed to be—and wanted to be—doing. "I'm going nowhere fast," she said. "If only I were loaded." Her parents had left her some money, but she had spent it. A Low Roller, she nevertheless liked big-ticket items, especially travel, on which she had spent a considerable sum.

Over the years, whenever she encountered an annoying obstacle, she was in the habit of saying to herself, "If only I were rich, I wouldn't have to put up with this." She had repeatedly tried to make that happen by always taking the highest-paying job offered her. It hadn't worked, and as time went by she finally gave up. "I'm not going to live forever," she said. "I'm going to do what *I* like from now on."

She said it out of bitterness at first, not really meaning it. But she was emotionally ready to at last make the words a reality. In the next three years, she did. She had spent seventeen fruitless and frustrating years as a publicist, and she finally had had enough.

Much to everyone's surprise, she abruptly requested, and received, a position in sales. She wanted to end the disputes about who deserved credit and wanted as well to get out of the office and start meeting people. "New people," she said, "different people, not the same old baggage."

That happened to an extent no one had anticipated. "She

was amazing," said the President of her firm as she began right from the start to bring in a number of major accounts the firm had been wooing for years without success. Within four years, her earnings had increased 260 percent and she was appointed Vice-President of the now much enlarged firm for which she had long worked.

A CRUCIAL BAROMETER

Like many others we studied, both Eileen and Charles had to grow a bit older, and hence mellow, before anything but conflict and dissatisfaction could be theirs. More precisely, what the passing years allowed them to do was lower their level of expectations to a more reasonable range and thus set the stage at last for success.

Eileen, Charles, and the overwhelming majority of people we studied were overmotivated; that is, far too eager to become rich. Where money is concerned, excessive motivation is an easy state to induce and a hard one to detect. Unlike a thermometer, which can readily be used to tell if your body temperature is too high, there is no comparable instrument to indicate you are emotionally pushing yourself too hard. Besides, if everyone else is doing it too, you might not notice it in yourself at all. Without an external standard of reference, it is difficult to know where you stand.

However, it is now clear that there is an invaluable internal barometer—the degree to which petty aspects of your work irritate you—which can be used for the purpose. Others may not be able to read it, but you can. In the concluding chapter, we'll see how to do so with a high degree of accuracy.

Not only can that barometer be used to assess whether you are asking too much of yourself, it will also tell you if you are heading in the wrong direction. Over and over again, it emerged that when someone was doing work which was meaningless to them, the trivial details connected with it were an annoyance. And the more meaningless, the more annoying the details.

Conversely, when they profoundly enjoyed their work, they were blind to the trivialities surrounding it. And the more they enjoyed it, the less likely they were to notice even discomforting trivialities which had to be attended to—details which others who were less involved found infuriating at worst, and painfully boring at best.

Bud Adams, the owner of the Houston Oilers football team, turned the $20,000 he had in 1946 into a personal fortune now worth well in excess of $100 million. Besides oil and gas, his main business, he also owns the nation's largest and most profitable Lincoln-Mercury dealership and one of the largest fully irrigated farms in the U.S., a 16,500 acre tract in California.

He told us, "The distinction between the lofty and petty aspects of your work is a dangerous trap. There is no such thing, in reality. You have to want to do—like doing—all of it. It's all yours, you know. You can't like some parts and be looking down your nose at the rest. You'll lose touch with what you're doing.

"The people I know who wanted to be associated only with grandeur, and who rejected all the gritty little things you have to do, eventually went down the drain. It's strange, but sometimes the trivia you have to do plugs you into your work better than the big things.

"Take, for instance, the checks we write. For years, I've balanced my own checkbooks. I've always had good bookkeepers. It wasn't a matter of not trusting someone. But it's hard to believe how much information about your business is sitting in those checks. As we got bigger, other people besides myself were signing them. Money was flowing out of here—in dozens of directions—that I never spent. My staff did. It's amazing how much you can learn about the people around you—and how your business is going—just by carefully going through those little slips of paper."

Then, in a brilliant comment, Adams added, "Look, the

more out of the ordinary what you are doing is, the more you *have* to be prepared to do it all. If you're running a standard business, turning out a standardized product, you can find someone who is good to do each job.

"But if you're trying something new, no one can really help you. At some point, you have to go it alone. And then, you have to do it all—the big and the little things—because only *you* know what you want the end result to look like.

"Scoffing at the lesser parts of your work will force your approach to be the traditional, the orthodox one. You'll never do anything that's unique, or different."

Instead of taking seriously what their internal barometer was loudly telling them, year in and year out, the vast majority of people we studied sought one remedy time and time again for their discomfort: they redoubled and then redoubled again their efforts to rapidly become rich. Their reasoning was simple: "What I'm doing now is tiresome and exasperating. But if I had money, I'd be free. I wouldn't have to do any of this."

In one way, the reasoning was valid. Had they been wealthy, they would undoubtedly have quit and tried doing something else. Money would indeed have helped to solve their problems at work, since it would have afforded them a measure of freedom and choice they thought they lacked.

So they tried desperately to become rich. The more annoyed they were, the harder they tried. And the harder they tried, the more annoyed they became. Upward the spiral of frustration climbed, until on the one hand, all they could think about was how damned irritating and petty their work was, and on the other, how intensely they wanted to become rich.

Now comes the truly awful part. Their focus on making a fortune made them not just resent, but despise the details of their work. Nevertheless, they expected it to ultimately make them wealthy. That was absolutely impossible. It will distress many to realize it, but work is 95 percent details. However, far from being appalled by that fact, those who became millionaires either delighted in the details or (more often) never noticed them at all. Since the pettier aspects constitute so large a portion of each day's work, in dismissing them with a sneer you may find your life has become empty.

Those who want something spectacular to happen, and hence who have contempt for all the little events which instead fill their hours, eventually find that nothing spectacular ever happens. Or will. Because those little details, quietly attended to, lead to the next step—and more details. And when those too are unconsciously handled, in time another step forward occurs—accompanied by more details, managed almost imperceptibly. Until from out of nowhere—or so it seems—success arrives, though rarely in the form in which it had originally been hoped for.

By the way, if it happens to you, you'll probably be among the last to know that it has. In all likelihood, you'll still have your mind immersed in the activity which was responsible for your success in the first place.

PART TWO

CHAPTER SEVEN

Investing in Yourself

After attempting for many years to locate satisfying jobs and not finding them, a sizable number of people have simply settled. "It's not what I want," said one, "but for the moment, it'll do." "All I do here is go through the motions," said another. "I don't care if the whole place falls apart," said a third, "as long as I get paid."

They are looking for meaningful employment, but there is nowhere they can go and ask for it, point-blank. So, they don't. Instead, they turn their frustration on their employer and their customers, and are often angry with everyone, including themselves. They know that no agency is responsible for helping them, and that even if it were, it would be faced with a difficult task. Work which is satisfying to one person might prove excruciatingly dull to another.

Those who are dissatisfied with their work thus aim their call for help at no one in particular. In essence, they make their request to—well, anyone who will listen. And what they say couldn't be simpler: "All I want is a really good job." It was easily the single most frequently heard complaint we encountered. Sometimes it was said directly to us, but for the most part, it was just said. In fact, it is now voiced so often, people who hear it barely react. As one said in reply, "Good, go find one." A second commented, "Oh yeah? What else is new?" The complaint is too stale and seemingly innocuous to warrant much in the way of a response.

Nevertheless, the statement, "All I want is a really good job," is one of the most dangerous sentences in the English language. Few requests currently cause so many Americans so much distress for so many years as this one does.

When you carefully explore what the last two words in the sentence mean to the person who has just uttered them, something remarkable emerges. By "good" it turns out they mean high-paying, not too strenuous, clean, and dignified, in that order. "I'd do dirty work," one said, "but I'd have to make plenty." "The harder I work," said a second, "the better I want to be paid." "It should be a prestige position," said a third. "I want to feel good about myself."

As for the word "job," take a guess as to how many of the people who eventually became millionaires thought of their work as "a job." Oh sure, they said "my job" often. We are all experts at attaching neat, acceptable labels to the things we do. Something may be of enormous personal importance to us, and just to make certain no one thinks we are crazy, we soft-pedal it.

For those who eventually became wealthy, it is fair to say that the word "mission" would be a more apt characterization of their involvement with their work than is "job." Forget the words they themselves use to project an image of normality. These people had been seized and were held tightly in the grip of their work to an extent which is difficult for anyone—including themselves—to imagine. "Consumed," as a description, barely does the situation justice.

We have already seen in Part I how difficult the vast majority of people are making matters for themselves in trying to go from Stage Two to Stage One, from first finding financial independence to subsequently locating an absorbing interest. What is being unwittingly asked for by someone who wants "a really good job" is even more radical. When all is said and done, they are asking someone to give them, simultaneously, Stage One *and* Stage Two satisfaction.

It is so unreasonable a request, almost everyone who begins to discover what the words mean quickly backs away from them. "I'm not sure what kind of work it'd be," said one. "I know I'm not looking for a handout." Not consciously, anyway.

The people asking for "really good jobs" aren't unemployed. Those we studied presently have annual incomes ranging from $9,600 to over $170,000, and the work they are doing is in an area of their own choosing. They hadn't taken "just any job," although that is indeed the way they have come to view the position they now hold.

There are a fair number of people who simply don't want to work. For them, no job will be suitable, no matter how interesting the activity might be to almost everyone else and how attractive a setting is provided in which to do it. Let's exclude them for the moment, and concentrate on the vastly larger number of people who would like very much to find what they call a "good job."

After many years of studying the topic, it can safely be said that no one can hand you Stage One satisfaction. That, you have to find yourself. Profound involvement in an area, activity, or field apparently always springs from sources deep within a person. Why someone likes an area and another does not, much less why the one who likes it subsequently becomes so caught up in it, is not very well understood. Perhaps in decades—or centuries—to come, it will be. What is necessary now, and it will be in the future too, is to accept your inclinations and give them their due, whatever their inner source.

But why would people prevent themselves from finding engrossing work in the first place? What would cause them to stifle such a desire (assuming the activity isn't dangerous, harmful, or illegal), especially since not finding it will impoverish their lives considerably?

WORK YOU AREN'T BEING PAID TO DO

A variety of factors enter the picture, but one occupies a dominant position. It has to do with the nature of modern occupations. Basically, when you work, you are being paid not to do things. In fact, almost everything, except the one at which your employer hopes you will eventually come to excel.

That may seem a very negative way of viewing work, but it sets the stage for some enormously positive changes to occur. The most important characteristic shared by those who did not succeed was that they accepted that restriction unthinkingly. Those who became wealthy, on the other hand, were better at following their noses, wherever that happened to take them. Paradoxically, people who became rich were far less accurate in their predictions of what they'd be doing ten, fifteen, and twenty years down the road than were those who failed.

In allowing themselves to try a variety of different approaches to their field, they finally hit upon the one which worked best for them. They weren't necessarily more ambitious, smarter, or more talented. Yet, in giving themselves the opportunity to locate what for them was the right angle of attack, they reaped a monumental bonus.

When people are well matched to their work, numerous facets of themselves are automatically mobilized which might otherwise never have been used. It is no illusion: the two seem made for one another, and are—everything the person is finds expression in his or her work. But precisely because the fit is such a good one, they become enormously *more* than their work. Vast areas of themselves remain in ready reserve, needed at certain times and not at others, waiting, if the time is right, to play an important supporting role.

When the match is that perfect, parts of the person are activated—even if they are never used—which until then had lain dormant. Is it any wonder the person succeeds almost without effort?

YOUR MOST IMPORTANT ASSET

If you are tempted to run out and spend your money at one of the many firms which say, "For $200 (or $2,000), we'll tell you what you're good at," please don't. Many are frauds. The rest, although perhaps well intentioned, are incapable of assisting you in finding what you want. The experiences in this area of the people we tracked are appalling.

The firms may on occasion have a customer who is so pleased with the services which were provided that he or she is willing to do a testimonial for them ("I was a $90 a week nothing, and people used to kick sand in my face. Now I earn $100,000 a year. . . ."), yet not one of the people we studied would. A thirty-three-year-old woman, unhappy in her sales position, who spent $1,600 to find out that she was "good in abstract reasoning" and can handle and "should meet top management," was furious. "I was no better afterward than before. And I was out the money." She was not alone. All told, during the two decades, the 1,057 uselessly spent more than $213,000 on such advice.

You don't need such firms. The irritation index you've got built into you, the extent to which you are annoyed by the pettier aspects of a position or project, will give you the best obtainable reading of what you really enjoy.

Since in working, you are being paid not to do a wide variety of things you otherwise would, that is the place to begin. Some of the activities your work now forces you to overlook may be the very ones you'd find most absorbing. And inasmuch as no one else is paying you to do them, you will have to pay yourself for doing them.

That is a concept very few people seem at ease with. Bert, an accountant, is a history buff. When he was asked what he thought of the idea of someone paying him to read a history book of his own choosing, he nearly became giddy with delight. Yet he was unwilling to consider paying himself to do the same. Sandy, a municipal employee, was similarly thrilled at the idea of being paid to compose the music and write the words for Broadway musicals, but felt foolish at the prospect of paying herself to do it. "It seems so narcissistic," she said uncomfortably.

Well, if they, as well as the others we studied, were discomfited by the thought of paying themselves to do the things they enjoy, what *would* they have done with any money given them? Forty-three percent—455 of 1,057—felt it was acceptable to spend it buying things: stereos, radar ranges, cars, carpets, and vacations. Ninety-four percent—992 of 1,057—thought that investing it was a good alternative, maybe the best one. Consumption or investment, those were the two distinct choices which sprang to mind.

And what kinds of investments were they talking about? Stocks, bonds, and real estate, primarily. Amazingly, we are back to Stage Two. They intend to use the $20,000 to make even more money, first. And when they finally have enough—whenever that is—they know without a shadow of a doubt what they'll do. As Bert put it, "*Then* I'd read, and write, history books." And Sandy? "At last I'll be able to do musicals."

Most of the multimillionaires we interviewed not only strongly disagree with Bert and Sandy, they also don't feel it is *ever* necessary to invest in other fields. As far as they're concerned, the best, and ultimately the most profitable, place to reinvest surplus income is in the area which produced the income in the first place.

Norman Lear, the producer of "All in the Family," "Maude," and a number of other extremely successful shows, put it very well when he told us, "What do I know about ranches? If I buy one and decide to go into the business of raising cattle or pigs, I'd have to hire an experienced professional to run it for me. The same with real estate and stocks.

"Before I know it, I'll have a bunch of people telling me what to do with my money. And I'll have to listen to them, because I'd be paying them for their expert advice. It just doesn't make sense to pay people to boss you around. *That* you can get for free. Your friends will be happy to do it for nothing."

Later he added, "*This* is the business I want to be in. Lucky for me the opportunities were steadily expanding. The communications field was exploding. I've had—and I'm having—no trouble finding good places *in this field* to invest the money I've made."

Thanks to the "Stage Two-first" orientation of the overwhelming majority of Americans, there are now armies of stockbrokers, land and condominium peddlers, gold and silver dealers, art, antique, and jewelry vendors, insurance and mutual fund sales agents, not to mention hucksters of get-rich-quick schemes, all of whom want whatever amount you have, no matter how small. And who, out of the goodness of their hearts, will bend over backward to make it convenient and easy for you to give them your money.

But to put it bluntly, if you only have $100,000 or less to invest, there is *no* place you can reasonably invest it. Except in yourself.

Buying stocks or real estate, and hoping they will skyrocket in value and make you rich, may at first glance seem appropriate. In the short run, if things go well, they may make you some money. Yet over the long term, the results indicate you won't do nearly as well using that route.

No matter how uncomfortable the thought makes you, the fact remains that *you* are your most important asset. That sounds terribly hackneyed and sugary, but we don't mean it in a gooey, inspirational way. Instead, it is a statement about the financial odds in your life. What the evidence clearly shows is that with, say, $5,000, $30,000, or $80,000 to invest, you are unlikely to become rich as a Stage Two investor. As a Stage One investor, you very well might.

CONSISTENCY

The lives of those who eventually became millionaires were characterized by prolonged periods during which they accidentally invested in themselves. What, then, prevented others who appeared to be doing the same from also getting there?

Howard and Jesse initially seemed quite similar. Both were the same age and wanted to be actors. Although they needed nonacting jobs to support themselves, they happily spent whatever it cost to take acting and voice lessons, and to buy tickets to plays. They also got together with friends to rehearse lines which stood little chance of being publicly heard, though it did afford them the practice they needed.

That did not continue. As their late twenties and early thirties rolled around, a decided difference emerged in the spending patterns of the two. Howard began devoting a much larger portion of the money he spent to creature comforts. "Decorating my apartment puts me in a happier frame of mind," he said. "I'm happier in a nice place."

We aren't suggesting he should have spent his money in a manner other than the one he did. For example, he may have concluded that other areas had finally become more important to him. But of great interest to us is that he didn't think so. He still wanted very much to be an actor. "So much so, I can *taste* it," he said. "I want to be up there." Moreover, he still remained convinced that acting would bring him the riches and recognition he sought.

Words and actions part company with surprising ease, not just in this example, but in hundreds of others we could cite. If our publicly declared goal is to become an actor, say, then it becomes necessary for us to make some effort in that direction or risk being called "full of hot air" or a "phony."

What happens, then, if we lose the desire? Do we tell others that our self-professed goal no longer seems so important? Do we tell ourselves? It was strange to see so many people pursuing goals they no longer cared about, mainly because they had portrayed themselves to their friends as being "well on their way" to success in the field. Having done so, any major changes would have required an explanation. And the explanation might not have sounded convincing enough. Better to stay with the old route than to risk being called a failure, or worse—in fact, the worst possible—inconsistent.

Being found inconsistent bothers many. They see it as extremely important to depict themselves as being the same person, with the same convictions, each time they encounter someone. Yet, we've already seen that those who became millionaires followed their occupational inclinations, wherever they led.

When asked about that, they too always tried to present their activities as being quite consistent. Nevertheless, they allowed their interests to carry them along, almost unconsciously. They unwittingly paid less attention to the shifts than they did to how those shifts aided them in getting or staying closer to their goal.

When Jesse was thus finally offered a part in a TV soap opera, he took it willingly. "I auditioned for it half asleep; I never thought I'd get it," he said. "It isn't my first choice. There are other acting jobs I'd rather have." But here, as always happened in the case of those who ultimately succeeded, he somehow recognized that if a door opened, maybe it was because he'd been knocking on it.

What was striking, however, was that it was Howard, not Jesse, who began talking up a storm about how much he was spending on developing himself. "My self-improvement program comes first," he said. "I want to be ready for anything." So much time and effort was going into getting ready to do something important, he seems to have forgotten what it was he was getting ready for.

That happens with a frequency which is astonishing. An endless number of times people became so hung up on the preliminaries to an event, they never got to the event at all. It was no accident that their conversation suddenly started becoming full of complaints about, as one put it, "all the trivial and idiotic obstacles that get in the way," because in fact, the nontrivial goal on the horizon had disappeared.

Thanks to the need for a public stance of consistency, those who grew tired of pursuing a particular picture of success usually did not say so. Instead, something remarkable happened: they began to pretend they had already achieved the success they once sought.

Struggle was no longer necessary. The goal which was originally a long distance away was at last at hand. They began to dress, think, and act as if any day—perhaps any minute—they would be given an award for outstanding performance in their field. The less time and money Howard thus spent on trying to become an actor, the more he began to imagine he was already an actor—a world-famous one, who would soon be asked to come and pick up his Academy Award. Fantasy was called upon to fill the growing void left by a waning reality.

It was often quite difficult to separate those who were losing interest in a field, but who were compelled by their public stance to continue on with it, from those who were highly impatient, and who wanted the success they knew one day would be theirs to be theirs now. Indifference and impatience were frequently indistinguishable because, in either case, it is easy to convince yourself that success is "just around the corner." By dressing "like a man of the theater," as Howard put it, he was able to make himself look much more like a solidly established, professional actor than Jesse did. Although Howard talked and looked the part, and readily persuaded everyone that he was "the real thing," it was Jesse who kept getting the little parts which eventually brought him a large part in a major motion picture.

Put simply, a growing loss of interest in a field acts as a detour only if you continue clinging to a rigid and outdated picture of what success in that field is supposed to look like. Let's glimpse at four examples.

Anne wasn't sure when it was she decided to become a

dancer, but her vision of what eminence in her field meant was as brittle as concrete: the audience leaps to its feet at the very moment your performance ends, shouting, "Encore, encore." After eight years of intense dedication, between the ages of fourteen and twenty-two, she began to be less absorbed. But like Howard, she then started to look even more like a dancer than she had during her period of maximum involvement.

As a little boy, Gary wanted to be a fireman, but as a third-year college student, he wanted to be a manager. He had an unclouded picture of what the position involved. "You get to boss people around," he said, "telling them to 'do this' and 'do that.'" After working for fourteen years at two airlines and not yet making it to the desired slot, his interest in the goal began to decrease. Paradoxically, he became more abrasive than ever. "I'm no longer an apprentice, you know," he said firmly. They hadn't made him the boss, so he decided to make himself one, much to the distress of the people below him.

Joann had always wanted to be an outstanding magazine editor and have all the benefits which in her mind automatically come with the position. As she originally put it, "You get to be interviewed on all the talk shows," and "are friends with everyone who is rich and famous," and also are "a trend-setter of opinions and attitudes."

After sixteen years of trying at three different magazines— "years of scratch and claw," she called them—she was clearly growing tired of the whole business. Strangely, the number of references she started making to wealthy and famous people she knew "as well as I know my own family" began to increase noticeably. People were thinking of putting her "on the talk show circuit," she said, where "I'll have a chance to tell people what's new and what it's all about." Some of her friends, who knew how fictional her stories had become, thought she was cracking up. "Not one word she says lately is the truth," said a longtime associate. Joann wasn't flipping out, she was acting out: success, according to her brittle view of it, had at last arrived.

ANTIQUATED IMAGES OF SUCCESS

And finally, Lenny had always wanted to be, as he put it, "a financier, like J. P. Morgan or Hughes or Getty." In his late teens and early twenties, he had a crystal-clear picture of what that entailed: "What you do is sit around and have meetings with other millionaires and billionaires." About what? "You buy and sell everything, and have people lighting your cigar and opening the door to your Rolls-Royce for you."

After graduate school, he was offered a job in the bond business and grabbed it. "I'm on my way," he said. "Nothing will stop me now." In the course of two decades, he became quite experienced at his job, and although his salary steadily increased, his emotional involvement with his work slowly decreased. He still continued to pay lip service to his "unstoppable rise to the top," as he described his inevitable future path. Now, though, he added a few props, each of which made it seem as though his "rise to the top" were already complete. A huge Lincoln Continental, "a better class of friends," as he called them, and even cigars, "because they do something for my image."

None of the examples we've been discussing is out of the ordinary. These are bright, hard-working people who have experienced a moderate degree of accomplishment and are now growing tired of their field. They aren't any less interested in success than they have always been, but they've come to dislike the field they once hoped would make them rich and famous. The rigid picture they have of success in their field is crippling them. They no longer want to do their work, but they do indeed want to live that picture.

Why an image of success in a particular field should have such a tenacious hold on young and not so young minds isn't clear. But it's always of someone else's success, someone from the past. A current picture would be entirely different, possessing no similarity to those old photos and depictions. This year's Nobel Prize in physics will probably not go to someone who resembles Albert Einstein, and the director of the year's best film will in all likelihood bear little resemblance to Ingmar Bergman.

Those who eventually became rich followed a surprisingly winding road, full of curves and sharp turns. But by allowing themselves to go where it took them, even if that meant straying far from petrified and antiquated images of "what success really means," they got there, anyway. No other route would have worked.

WORK AND SEX

Petrified pictures of success are an important detour—one which pulls you off the road when it bends—but there is another, one which many found themselves taking.

"If you enjoy something, you shouldn't have any trouble getting yourself to do it." The sentence sounds reasonable, and the large majority of people we studied considered it valid. Yet the fact remains that we often have to push ourselves a bit, to get started, before the enjoyment takes over and carries us the rest of the way. In fact, both the people who succeeded as well as those who failed often required an initial boost to get going. The two groups did not differ greatly in this respect.

They did, however, differ significantly in their willingness to give themselves that needed first push. Some even said to themselves, "I don't feel like doing it right now, but I know once I get started, I will." Others didn't think about it, they just did it. "Time to get to work," one mumbled. Still others felt sorry for themselves momentarily. "Poor me," said one. "I have to do this thing [which I love]." Whether they used mechanical means or emotional ploys, one way or another those who eventually became millionaires displayed an ability to get themselves moving, in spite of an initial reluctance to do so.

What, then, is the detour taken by those who did poorly? It is contained in its clearest form in the following, frequently heard comment: "If I don't feel like doing it, it must be because I don't want to." Common sense tells us that that must be true, yet like much of what passes for common sense, it is not only false, it is a recipe for failure. Almost without exception, those who leaped to the conclusion that they lacked interest in something merely because they had difficulty getting "into it" made a costly mistake.

This is a major matter, a judgmental error which had significant long-term consequences. And perhaps the most illuminating way to see that it is indeed false is to examine the issue sexually instead of financially. The subject of masturbation sheds a much needed light here.

After the publication of the Kinsey reports in the late 1950s, a frequently encountered wisecrack was that "98 percent of Americans had masturbated and the other 2 percent were liars." Masturbation is indeed a standard component of human sexual behavior, and fortunately, the absurd strictures with which the nineteenth century surrounded the practice have largely disappeared, though schoolchildren still repeat them for amusement ("It grows hair on your palm," "makes you go blind," etc.).

Nevertheless, there is an aspect of masturbation which is very easily overlooked. Since attaining an orgasm is the point of the activity, what occurs during the early moments passes unnoticed. Yet there is a crucial focusing phase, in which the person first starts to seriously concentrate on the matter at hand, so to speak: an initial step, in which the relevant thoughts and erotic images are gathered.

Three hundred and sixty-one people who monitored the length of the initial focusing phase reported times which ranged from four to seventy-five minutes. The effort to note the time taken undoubtedly increased it, since it introduced an extraneous factor not usually present. But most claimed the times reported to us were typical, and they averaged approximately twenty-one minutes.

Why then should an initial focusing phase where your work is concerned be viewed with such distrust, as indicating a probable lack of interest in the activity?

Is it your view that, because there was an initial, thought-gathering period required for masturbation, few were really interested in the activity? Those who were surveyed certainly didn't feel that way: only 4 percent—13 of 361—agreed with that conclusion. The overwhelming majority simply took it for granted that they couldn't just "jump into it" (though on occasion they indeed did), and got started, anyway, perhaps slowly and haltingly.

Granted, there are significant differences between work and sex. Yet you probably won't be surprised to hear that the people we studied made more references to masturbation when discussing their work then they did to any other image. The enormous number of masturbatory references isn't endlessly meaningful (people use sexual metaphors to describe all kinds of nonsexual activities), but it's no accident either, and should alert us to an important inclination: we allow ourselves to be scared far more quickly and easily than we allow ourselves to have a good time, particularly where our work is concerned.

No doubt that inclination helped keep us alive for millions of years. Whatever its survival value in the past, however, it is now less a help than a hindrance. Those who took an initial reluctance to get to work as indicating a lack of interest in their work failed significantly more often than did those who simply accepted a thought-and-image-gathering phase as standard and who "got into" their work any way they could.

Only when they were deeply involved in it, and had repeatedly been so, could they accurately judge how much they enjoyed it, and hence how effective it would be in accidentally getting them to where they in fact wanted to go.

CHAPTER EIGHT

Socializing: Why Bother?

If the people we studied could get a product they needed more cheaply from a reputable stranger, they usually bought it rather than pay a higher price to a friend. Similarly, when they needed medical, dental, or legal services, they told us they preferred someone highly qualified whom they didn't know personally to someone less qualified whom they knew well. Price and performance mattered, and friendship alone was simply not enough.

Yet they also told us that they thought socializing would work miracles for them. In fact, they felt it was one of the best ways they could invest in themselves. For some reason, we apparently don't expect people to be as critical of us in business as we are of them. Hence when we socialize, we are nothing if not optimistic.

Let's look at some examples.

KNOCKING'EM DEAD

Roberta was outstanding at it. As one of her friends aptly commented, "She could strike up a conversation with a corpse." She did indeed seem able to talk easily with anyone. Her first jobs were as a model, and she was told more than once that her friendly, outgoing manner helped her get some repeat bookings she might otherwise not have. A High Roller, most of the money she made was soon spent. In her view, every penny used for the purposes of partying was an investment. But the conclusion hadn't been reached by analysis and arithmetic, it was simply an article of faith: "In this business, you *have* to know people. The more, the better."

Although she enjoyed socializing continually, it was exhausting. "I don't know which is harder," she quipped, "my work or my being out all night." Nevertheless, she felt it would have to continue if she were ever to get where she wanted to go. After nine years of modeling and a few TV commercials, she decided to try for the position of spokeswoman for a nationally known product line. The decision made her redouble her socializing efforts. "There are advertising and network people I need to know," she said, and there was little doubt in her mind that by partying she could not only meet them, but would be certain to leave a memorable impression, as well. "When I'm 'out on the town,'" she said, "I'm unforgettable."

Like the majority of people we studied, Roberta was basically in the business of selling herself. Not sexually, as you might think; sleeping around played a rather minor role. To her, it was far more important that everyone know who she was, find her awe-inspiring and want to pay her, too, just for being around. "I want to knock 'em dead every time I walk into a room," she said with determination, "and cash in on being able to do that." Promoting a name-brand product, both on camera and off, seemed to her a perfect way to realize her dream.

As part of an aggressive attempt to meet some of the advertising account executives who she thought could assist her, she got a friend to help her crash a party. The ad people she had hoped to meet were indeed there, and so was a well-known singer. "I killed two birds with one stone," she said. She asked for and was given the opportunity to try for the role, which she correctly guessed they were in a hurry to fill. And one of the singer's associates invited her to dinner the following week.

Much to her dismay, she did not get the part. She had been one of two finalists left, out of more than thirty who were seriously considered. "I just don't understand," she said angrily. "I've got a great face, a good body, and I can sell anybody, anything." Far from losing hope, though, she decided to ask the singer's friend, and if necessary the singer directly, to put her "in touch with people who are well connected and who will recognize what I can do for them." The matter had a certain urgency in her view. "I'm running out of time," she said. "I'm thirty-four and need something stable."

After dating the singer's friend on and off for fourteen months, he asked her to marry him. She was both amused and horrified. "Poor fool," she said, "doesn't he understand we're just friends?" She hastened to dump him and temporarily tied up instead with a wealthy man ten years her senior, who is interested in helping her form a marketing firm of her own. They have been together for the last four years, but the idea has remained at the conversation stage.

Similarly, John wanted to be a dancer, and right from the start was convinced that his chances of success would be bettered if he could become friends with the management of the dance company. When he was nineteen, he became a member of the corps of one of the world's foremost dance ensembles. Although he rehearsed diligently, he wanted to move up fast, and viewed socializing with his superiors as the shortcut he was looking for.

What was most remarkable about John was his ability to work himself into the good graces of the soloists, principals, and management of his company without making it seem as if he wanted anything from them at all. He, like many others we studied, had a practiced ease in the presence of such people. His desperation certainly had not disappeared, but he had perfected the art of hiding it completely at such moments. They had to offer. He knew he couldn't ask. Nevertheless, he was confident that sooner or later they would.

The fact that he rarely accepted their assistance—and instead usually offered them his—succeeded. They began inviting him to dinner at their homes and took him up on many of his offers, for example, to help them do household repair and redesign tasks, such as repainting a room or shopping for furniture. In spite of the skill he displayed at making people feel he wanted nothing from them, he dropped them promptly as soon as they in fact had nothing to offer. As their fortunes rose and fell, so did the degree to which they interested him. Proceeding quietly when slipping into or out of someone's life, he was able to avoid having his ambitions detected.

He had been able to remain a member of the company for eight years, in part because of his maneuvering. But in a field in which someone who is thirty is considered to be of an advanced age, he knew it was time to start making alternative plans. Utilizing his position as a member of a famous dance company, he began for the first time to turn his attention increasingly to people outside the world of dance. One, a restaurant-and-bar owner, thought that John's "elegant style and impeccable manners," as he put it, would expand the bar's clientele. Fond of John personally, completely convinced that here at last was someone who wanted little, if anything, from him, he gave John 25 percent ownership in the bar, and in two others, as well, expecting him in return to bring in new and different customers. That happened, but after six years of slow expansion and modest profits, far less than anticipated, he bought John out for $65,000. John went on to establish a similar pairing in another town, capitalizing on the experience he had gained during the six years.

There are many other Robertas and Johns we could look at, but these two are noteworthy, for although they do the same things others do, they handle themselves far more slickly than most. Almost everyone who met them was indeed impressed, at least initially. What we need to ask then is this: How effective are such techniques, not just as used by the Robertas and

Johns, but as a tool employed by a wide variety of people who are trying to become rich?

Roberta and John were unable to go as far as they wanted because they were overdoing it. Some who knew them noticed something of a pattern to their behavior, and even suggested that less socializing and more self-development would have been more productive.

To many, however, there is no room here for splitting hairs. That was the view of the people we studied who were in sales. Tom, an insurance salesman, felt that socializing *was* his business. "First off, it gets me new clients," he said, "and since I'm in the business of catering to these people, it helps keep them happy." Analogous comments were made by people employed selling everything from cars to legal services. It is an important point: When is socializing a normal and expected part of being in a particular business, and when is it being used for the purposes of climbing?

Strangely enough, while it was difficult for us to tell by merely watching what each person did, they themselves generally knew which was which. Many were so skilled at presenting themselves as being someone's friend, we often weren't certain whether or not they were being sincere. Nevertheless, they themselves could usually decide.

Their decision, however, was affected significantly by whether they were a High, Low, or No Roller. The more of a High Roller someone tended to be, the less they were able to distinguish between friends and business acquaintances. On the other hand, those who were Low, and especially No Rollers, were much more definite about whom they liked and whom they were using for financial purposes.

One of the ways in which that fascinating fact emerged is this: High, Low, and No Rollers were asked to list the people they had frequent contact with, and put "business" or "friend" next to each person's name. As the years passed, those lists, filled out regularly, proved surprising. It was common for people on them to move from the "business" to the "friend" category, and vice versa. But there were significantly more such shifts on the lists provided by the High Rollers. In many instances, names regularly bounced back and forth between the two categories.

High Rollers are clearly confused, but it is confusion with a purpose. They enjoy receiving money in clumps, and like spending it the same way, without accompanying thought. The salespeople we studied, for instance, unwittingly found themselves unable to take the distinction seriously. For they wanted to do business with all their friends, and they wanted everyone they did business with to be their friend. There is nothing particularly out of the ordinary about that; it is a traditionally American way of doing business.

What it should tell us, however, is that the more of a High Roller someone is, the more inclined they will be to spend money socializing, even if it isn't going to generate any income for them. That is simply the financial part of their style of personal expressiveness, and needless to say, in most cases it does indeed result in some business. We should add that in case there was no one around they felt like socializing with, they were strongly inclined to spend the money on clothes.

Now we can ask the question again: To what extent are people investing in themselves when they spend money socializing?

The answer is that if you are a High Roller, you are going to do it anyway. Nothing you read here is likely to affect the way in which you spend. But in the next section, we'll see that it is possible to get far more for your money than most people now do, regardless of the tightness or ease with which you spend your money.

"WHAT DO I DO FOR AN ENCORE?"

If the people you meet socially are to be of any real benefit to you in business, you will somehow have to win their respect. That they come to like you is all well and good. But people often told us that although they were fond of one person, they preferred doing business with another, more competent than the first.

This is the place where socializing was supposed to help, yet it is the point at which most people stumbled and fell. They were convinced they could make a more solid case for themselves in a social setting than they could through their work. And they could do so more quickly, as well. Many commented, "How do I know people will even get to see my work?", whereas in face-to-face conversation they counted upon being asked, "What do you do?", and if it was someone they already knew, "How's it going?"

The thinking was sound, and hence the fact that it didn't produce the anticipated results was puzzling. The number of socially skilled manipulators we were following was large: some were in sales, some not; some were High Rollers, others were Low or No Rollers. At least one should have been capable of achieving success using social connections, yet none did. Although we had originally expected to find plenty of people getting to the top through sex and socializing, there wasn't one.

The reason soon became clear. For instance, after Tom, the insurance salesman, had sold everyone in his circle all the policies he could, he asked himself, "What do I do for an encore?" Enormously social, he became even more so. And it did work, to some extent. It was producing a decent annual income, but as Tom knew only too well, it was never going to make him rich.

Tom, and people in other areas of sales, quickly discovered that socializing can become expensive. Not that he seriously objected. "I've *got* to locate more customers," he said, laughing. "By the time I finish wining and dining the ones I've already got, I'll have given them back everything I made from them."

To High Rollers like Tom, this was a typical—and satisfying—bit of confusion. When socializing, they rapidly lost track of how much they were making or spending (something, you'll recall, they do rather easily) and that the presence of so many people (friends?, customers?) must mean that the money is just rolling in.

The social whirl produced a feeling of exhilaration which escalated effortlessly. After all, the more money someone made for you, the more appropriate it was to socialize with them—and spend money on them. Why keep track? Things have to be going well. As Tom said, "Socializing *is* my business." Continually surrounded by people, he knew he must be growing rich fast.

Nevertheless, the party always ended for High, Low, and No Rollers on the same note: where to generate more business? Socializing produced only a limited income. Having peddled all the cars, insurance, stocks, bonds, and burial plots they could, those who were seeking additional income quickly realized what the next step would have to be: start doing business with a much wealthier individual or corporate customer. Climbing wasn't evil, it was a necessity once you had exhausted your friends.

That is what Roberta and John felt forced to do. They each had plenty of friends, but both were well aware that they would have to befriend people in higher circles if they were ever to get ahead.

A CHANCE TO "SHOW'EM"

If everyone in time realized their friends couldn't make them rich, why didn't their attempts to climb work? With so large a portion of the populace trying, some should have succeeded at becoming wealthy by befriending an appropriately powerful person. There are, after all, a fair number of stories to that effect constantly in circulation. However, if our results are at all indicative, the tales are fictional, at worst, and severely distorted, at best.

What typically happened to those in a hurry to become rich, and who latched onto someone in a position to help them, was this: they were given a chance, not a cashier's check for $1 million. That golden opportunity soon thereafter produced a moment of truth.

Diane, for instance, wanted to be a singer. It took a great deal of maneuvering, but she finally became firmly entrenched in a circle of professional recording artists. Much to the envy of her old friends, who suddenly realized that she had managed, as one put it, "to swing a sweet deal for herself" by getting solo billing at a top nightclub. She, like John, had intentionally accumulated a lot of social IOUs, but unlike John, now openly asked for payment. "If you really want to help me, get me every big-time agent, reviewer, and producer in the business," she said. "Make sure they are *there* that night."

Many were. But the reviews of her debut weren't at all what Diane had expected. Most said she wasn't ready. Some said she'd never be. Her interest in singing waned significantly in the subsequent months, and she returned to her job as a receptionist. We thought the stinging reviews and absence of additional offers might have played a role. "Nope," she said, "I got what I wanted," and she brought out a huge photo album, filled with hundreds of pictures taken that night. Every well-known figure who had been present was in at least one, with her. Diane still sings, at home, but the closetful of elaborate outfits she had bought in anticipation of her debut ("I wasn't sure until opening night which one I was going to wear") were sold some time ago.

Like many others, Mel, our next instance, told us repeatedly that all he needed was "a break." "If only someone would give me a chance," he said, "I'd show them." He had been working for a distributor of tools, sold primarily to hardware stores. Having gotten to know the company's operations thoroughly during his nine years there, he wanted to go into competition with his boss. The company was in the business of importing a product line, made to its specifications in the Far East. Mel didn't mind the fact that his firm manufactured none of the products it sold, and merely had its name stamped on whatever it imported. But he was convinced that at least some of the items—screwdrivers, wrenches, and pliers—could be made more cheaply here. "I know how to do it," he said, "and my boss doesn't."

The amount of financial backing Mel needed was substantial. "Getting the thing off the ground is going to cost over $300,000," he said, and during the next four years he set out to raise it. "I'm going after everyone who has money," he stated, and then proceeded to join a yacht club, as well as a country club, which, as he put it, "gives me access to the golf and tennis people." "It cost me a bundle to join," he said, shaking his head, "but I'll get it back, in spades."

He did. He made his case passionately and with conviction, particularly to a group of three investors he had met through a sailing acquaintance of his. One of the three was persuaded by the knowledge of the tool business Mel displayed, and with $200,000 from the three and additional financing from a bank, Mel was soon in business.

The company performed adequately during its first thirty months of operation, but Mel grew increasingly indifferent to the whole project. At last, it was obvious why. "*I* showed him," he said, referring to his old boss. Mel had achieved what he set out to do, and fourteen months later his company went bankrupt. He now works for a major domestic manufacturer of carpenters' and mechanics' tools.

These two examples and many others had certain features which commonly recurred. First, there was a desperate desire on someone's part to be given an opportunity to do something. Second, using social connections, they got it. And third, having gotten it, they soon lost interest in the activity. In short: someone yearned to do something, but once they actually tried, their deep desire gave way to smug satisfaction and a "Yep, I did it."

Why? What would make people who had spent years organizing their professional, social, and at times sex lives around "being given a chance" walk away from an area which had previously meant so much to them. We witnessed the event regularly, but what was startling was how little it took for people to feel they had "done" something. In many cases a day, or a night of it, was enough.

As other examples were examined, the underlying factors emerged. For instance, it was revealing to note the amounts of time each activity took. On the one hand, we kept track of the "yearning and maneuvering," and on the other, the work itself that people fervently claimed they wanted to do.

It wasn't even close: there was so much more of the former than the latter, we were finally forced to conclude that there are a substantial number of people spending their lives "yearning and maneuvering," but who are doing so under the guise of "If only someone would give me an opportunity, I'd work like a demon."

We need to be careful here to avoid attributing sinister motives to people who didn't have them. No doubt, a good percentage simply grew tired of one field and instead decided to try another. That can't be the whole story, however. For once they were active in a new area, they again spent far more of their time yearning than working.

Although most were reluctant to admit it, many did openly acknowledge that they loved the wheeling and dealing most. Trying to raise money for their projects was exciting, in and of itself—more so, in fact, than the projects themselves. And in almost all the instances, more than just money was at stake.

ACCEPTANCE, REVENGE, AND SUPERIORITY

An equally if not more significant issue was acceptance. People who yearned for an opportunity wanted a chance to publicly be "at my best," so that, as one put it, "the world could sit up and say, 'What do you know? So-and-so is the real thing, after all.'"

Two other factors were also significant. Revenge and superiority. Telling yourself, "I'll show them," may make it sound as if the achievement is your principal focus, but in fact it is much the same as saying, "I'll get even with them." Why

Roberta, John, Diane, and Mel felt like getting even, we don't know. But since their actions were motivated in good part by vengeful feelings, once they felt they had "showed'em," they could then drop the project. And did.

The last factor, superiority, was plainly present in the comments often made. "They've got money, so they think they're wonderful," and, "I'm not going to beg them just because they have what I need." Although many realized their friends couldn't make them rich, they had mixed feelings about having to ask someone who had more money or power than they for aid.

The five factors combined easily, and explosively. Almost all the people who dedicated themselves to gaining acceptance and then assistance from others they viewed as superior succeeded, at least in part. Using manipulative skills which had been developed and refined to an awesome extent, they presented themselves and their plans so convincingly, they conned everyone, including themselves.

The maneuvering may have been enjoyable, but it was also monumentally grim. To begin with, just as High Rolling salespeople had to do, it was necessary for unwitting con artists to entertain their clients. But only about half the skilled manipulators we are discussing were High Rollers. The rest found the process unnatural, not exhilarating, and were forced to carefully watch their own every word and action. Calculating every move was a continuing strain, but was absolutely essential, since this time the stakes were a lot higher than a simple sale. And it made them want their revenge and their reward all the more.

They usually got it, but it took many years. Since it was necessary to first befriend the powerful people who were in a position to be of use, it was difficult to rush the process. Friendship blossoms slowly, and there was always the danger of asking the question too pointedly, or too soon.

For instance, Joyce tried for eleven years to support herself at a level far above what she was able to afford. But she was always able to find men, usually considerably older than she, who were willing to help her. As one put it, "She is beautiful, and has everything I've always wanted in a woman."

Similarly, Bill was good at finding women who, as he put it, "are looking to help me further my career." It was never quite clear to us what that career was, since it kept changing, but whatever it happened to be at any given time, he always succeeded in finding somebody to help him "further it."

There are good reasons for us to look carefully at how Joyce and Bill operate. First, there are far more of both of them than most people imagine. And second, neither of them saw themselves as parasites. Joyce unswervingly claimed, year in and year out, for two decades, that she wanted above all to be an actress, and if not that, to run her own business. Bill said he wanted to be an artist, or else "be part of a business of which I can be proud." Although between them they went through a sizable number of patron-partners (seventeen in all, each lasting an average of twenty-two months), they were both at pain to repeatedly point out that they "resent handouts." "I don't want anything I'm not entitled to," said Bill. "I don't need anything from you, or anyone else," Joyce was fond of telling her partners. Nevertheless, unconsciously, but diligently, both remained in constant pursuit of the same goal. "I want to be financially independent," said Bill firmly.

The way they attempted to achieve that goal was breathtakingly bold. Both essentially told a variety of partners, "I have much less money than you do. And it bothers me to keep on asking you for small amounts. Why don't you give me a bulk sum, so I won't feel dependent upon you?" Though they said it subtly and tactfully, their partners were usually stunned at the idea. Some, however, were struck by a peculiar logic they sensed the words possessed, and one forked over $70,000. Another transferred $50,000, saying, "There, now you won't feel you have to compromise yourself with me."

It is of major importance that none of the Joyces or Bills we studied was able to merely leave the large sum they had just received in the bank. They had many debts to pay, some of which were sizable. Their partners, after all, were wealthy people with an expensive life-style, which was a good part of what attracted the Joyces and Bills to them to begin with. The money they received was given them with the tacit understanding that it would be used for the purpose of "keeping up." Dressing stylishly and eating well were the minimum expected. Anything they could do to make themselves more appealing or interesting was also a valid expenditure.

Both obviously enjoyed it, and neither complained. What is amazing, however, and a testimonial to the remarkable skill they had in this department, long after they had parted company with past partners, they remained able to call a good many of them, and with a suitable sob story, get another bulk sum "to help preserve their independence."

KEEPING UP WITH YOUR CLIENTS

There was one problem faced by every individual we've discussed thus far in this chapter, and none solved it. All wanted to become rich, and openly said so. Yet, not one did. None even came close.

Their lavish life-style made many observers conclude that these people must already have made their first million and be well on their way to a second. Nonetheless, the amount they had in the bank, or in stocks, bonds, and real estate, was modest or marginal throughout the two decades we followed them. Many who were jealous criticized them, calling them "bloodsuckers," "parasites," and "climbers," but the fact remains that, in terms of the amount of money they succeeded in accumulating, they hadn't climbed anywhere, and hence had to constantly be on the lookout for ways to make more.

In short, your friends can indeed put you in business—or expand the one you now have—but only moderately. Once you have sold everyone you know a product or service, the pressure will begin building for you to expand your social circle. It isn't all that difficult to do, but it isn't likely to dramatically increase your income.

First of all, socializing with potential clients costs money—and the wealthier they are, the more expensive the process will be. Second, it takes time, years in many instances. You can't simply say "Hello" to someone and start selling. So many people have had that happen to them, and were annoyed, they are ready to recoil more quickly the next time someone tries to repeat it.

Socializing proved to be an expensive and slow-growth route, when it was successful at all. Although almost everyone considered it an investment, few attempted to figure out what the net financial return they received was. Had they done so they'd have realized, much to their surprise, they lost, not made money. It turns out they would have stood a better chance of coming out ahead had they "invested" in a roll of the dice in Las Vegas. The income their socializing produced rarely came close to even covering the expenses they had incurred.

They were able to mask the underlying arithmetic by saying that the get-togethers were "just for fun." Yet that can't have been wholly true. For when we asked, "Would you have chosen to socialize with that person if the two of you had, from the start, been prohibited from doing business together?" they usually replied, "No."

A second, and more disturbing, way in which people avoided facing the underlying financial facts was to not put a value on their own time. "I'm not at work now," one said about getting together on a weekend socially with someone to whom she hoped one day to sell some cosmetics. "I was off duty, then," said another about an evening he had spent "buttering up," as he put it, someone whom he thought might later help him get a promotion.

Like an enormous number of others, these two were using their leisure hours for what were basically business purposes. Let's hope they really had the good time they say they did, because in the vast majority of such instances they, and others like them, would have come out far ahead financially had they instead devoted the time to moonlighting at a second job, even if it paid only half as well as their daily work did.

Joseph Brooks, the Chairman and Chief Executive Officer of Lord & Taylor, had some striking observations on this score. He told us, "There is a serious defect in the thinking of someone who wants—more than anything else—to become rich. As long as they don't *have* the money, it'll seem like a worthwhile goal. Once they do, they'll understand how important other things are—and have always been. But by then, it will be too late.

"You have to define what it is that's going to make you tingle. Find work that makes you glad to be alive. The two—a tingling feeling and money—go together. You *can* have them both. The first will lead you to the second.

"Do the best you can every day. Forget about the future. The word 'future' has become a disease. You have to work hard today to even have a tomorrow. I see dozens of capable men and women who worry so much about what's going to happen to them the next day, they're not part of today. It only looks like they're right in front of you. They're not. They're off somewhere, living in the future. Only when you're embedded in *today* can you force yourself to stretch and do more than you ever thought you could. Greed and anxiety are preventing everything that's best in them from rising to the surface.

"If you love your work, and do it well, someone will spot that. It takes a lot of people to help you move up, and you're not going to be able to step over *all* of them. Let the quality of your work do it for you.

"Competitive people make the good feelings which should prevail around you disappear. They act as if they're in love with themselves, but the holes they keep digging for everyone else, they themselves wind up falling into.

"The ones I've met who want praise, and grab someone else's in order to get it, are doing something awful—to themselves. They think it'll work, but I've watched: they'll be neither happy nor successful. Recent university graduates are always flabbergasted to hear it, but there are a lot of people in top management positions who feel the same way I do. I believe everyone who's really good should do *better* than I did. I expect them to benefit from what I've learned, and get there faster. I want every 'pupil' of mine to make more money than I did—and at an earlier age.

"Socializing won't help make that happen, not with me and not with anyone else in my position. The horrible thing about the business-social climbers I've seen is that they are *voluntarily* choosing to spend so much of their time with people they dislike. What a horrible thing that is to do to yourself. Do enough of it, you won't even know who you are—or what it is you really want to accomplish."

When all is said and done, socializing for business purposes is, in and of itself, work. But instead of being steady employment, it is a series of brief jobs.

That is part of what many found attractive about it from the start. Only a handful of hours are consumed each time. An attempt to "get in good" with and then make a sale to (or get money or a promotion from) someone may have felt like a day's work, but it usually took far fewer hours than are contained in a normal workday.

The trouble was that the person's regular work was often neglected in the process. In many instances, people were uncertain as to how valuable socializing with business associates was, and did it mainly because, as they put it, "it can't hurt." The fact that they didn't particularly like someone didn't prevent them from pursuing that person if they thought the person would ultimately be of use.

What frequently happened is that they wound up spending a considerable portion of their nonwork hours with people they could barely stand. "But it will pay off one day," said one. "If you want to get ahead," said another, "this is the way to do it." And a third: "I want them to know I'm as good as they are."

What our results clearly reveal, however, is that the most important consequence of wanting to prove something to someone is that once you've done it, you are likely to forget the matter. That is, you're probably going to persist only as long as you feel you haven't yet "shown'em" to your satisfaction.

Nevertheless, "showing'em" has nothing to do with work, and instead usually wound up replacing it. A deep desire for acceptance, superiority, revenge, and money may make someone's wheeling and dealing temporarily meaningful. But conning people, no matter how well you do it, causes you to substitute a sequence of short-term goals for the one long-term goal responsible for making people wealthy: finding work you enjoy and accidentally persisting in doing it.

Jane Cahill Pfeiffer is the Chairman of the Board of NBC and is paid over $400,000 a year. In a series of fascinating comments, she told us:

"It was a great awakening for me when I first had to do something at work I couldn't, because the people who usually helped me happened not to be around at the time. It was a great lesson in being on your own—and in humility. It's not easy, but you have to be willing to make mistakes. And the earlier you make those mistakes, the better. In the beginning, your blunders may loom large in your mind, but they're not very costly to your firm. Later, after you've been promoted a number of times and have more responsibility, they'll be bigger, and they can badly hurt both you and your firm. What you overlooked earlier catches up with you later.

"The financial, legal, personnel, and communications areas —the 'softer sides' of your business—are just as important as any product you turn out. And if yours is a firm which only provides services, rather than producing products, the *product* of your business is those services. Socializing, no matter how well you do it, is no substitute for doing a good job in each of those areas. I'm aware that socializing is one of many short-cuts people have used to get ahead. But at *some* point they run out of the ability they need in order to operate at the level they've so cleverly attained. They used their social skills to climb, but once the pressure builds up, they're going to be found out. They're in over their head, and sooner or later, it shows.

"There are people with 'hard elbows,' and there are those with 'soft elbows'—people who try to knock you out of the way and grab your credit, and those who do it gently, if at all. You have to use 'hard elbows' on rare occasions—specifically when you're dealing with someone who's doing that to you—but even then, you have to do so *very* judiciously.

"A strategy of trying to bump others out of the picture, playing games, taking advantage of others, eventually gets found out, for two reasons. Either you are given an assignment you're not really capable of coping with, or else you become too open about what you're doing. Either way, you'll finally be stopped in your tracks.

"Personal qualities matter, and socializing—in the sense of being friendly—is necessary. You do have to work with other people. But no game or gimmick can substitute for performance, regardless of how socially slick you are. I take—and have always taken—a very simple view of this matter: if people perform well, and assume responsibility for themselves, they'll succeed, ultimately. It's great to use all the tricks of your trade, but you better stick to the fundamentals and learn your business just as well as you possibly can. I always get very involved in what I'm doing, and that has always made me eager to learn, made me welcome every opportunity I could find to do still better. The farther up the ladder you go, the more will be demanded of you. There's just no escaping that. It's not just your classmates, your peers, whose performance counts. The world really is much smaller now, and increasingly, there is going to be pressure from foreign competitors. Beating out those around you just won't do. If you get to the top using tricks, instead of by concentrating on developing your abilities, your position is going to be very shaky. Even if you succeed, you'll have failed."

SOCIALIZING YOUR WAY TO FAME AND FORTUNE

Social contact with people you enjoy is important, particularly if you are active in an area of work you find absorbing. And nothing we've said here is intended to diminish its importance. But the amount of intentionally fuzzy thinking about socializing done by people who are anxious to become wealthy is nothing short of staggering.

To some extent, especially in the case of High Rollers, the confusion is genuine. But many others made themselves into synthetic High Rollers, and calculatedly attempted to freely socialize in what they hoped would be a very profitable manner. It almost never was. And if you are to avoid wasting years, and even decades, which the process of partying for business purposes can easily consume, you need to stop and consider whether your time and energy are being well spent.

If you enjoy someone's company, by all means get together with that person. But if you think socializing is a good investment, and will one day help make you rich, you should know that, try as we might (for we too wanted to believe it), we couldn't find one instance in which socializing generated fame or fortune.

Socializing is, at best, piecework and temporary employment. And without the accidental persistence produced by absorption in work you enjoy, the chances of becoming rich turned out to be nil.

CHAPTER NINE

Easy Come, Easy Go—
Those Who Made Fortunes
and Lost Them

Although the people we studied had never been wealthy, they certainly wanted to be. Some, however, did manage to make it from rags to riches. Starting from modest beginnings, 83 succeeded in eventually becoming worth in excess of $1 million. Eleven of the 83 then managed to lose it. Astonishingly, three of the eleven went on to repeat the process. It is worth our while to see who the eleven were, and how they managed to make—and lose—$1 million. And then, in some instances, do it again.

SELLING THE RIGHT PRODUCT

Ben doesn't think of himself as one of the world's greatest salesmen, but he is. He would have considered it impolite, and even irrelevant, to say such a thing to someone to whom he was trying to make a sale. Instead, he always talked about the product or plan he was selling at the moment.

Ben held a variety of jobs after majoring in sociology in college—and detesting it—for three years, before dropping out. All the positions were in sales, even though in not one of the cases had he been hired as a salesman. "He was a natural," said his second employer. "He kind of drifted into selling for us." "Why did he leave?" we asked his ex-boss. "Oh, he had big plans," he explained, "and we were just too small."

Ben became a stockbroker during the sixties, when it sometimes seemed that everyone was either a broker or a customer. "Is there any other business?" he asked rhetorically, when first applying for the job. At the time, the answer in his case clearly was "no." His skill at getting people to come up with money, in the first place, and then give it to him for investing, soon became obvious. The income he earned soared as the market did. But in 1969–70, the game ended for him, as it did for many others. He needed a new group of customers, since he had left the old ones for the most part bankrupt. The wildly speculative stocks were the ones he had made his reputation playing, and when they plummeted, most never to recover, it was necessary for him to hunt up a new reputation elsewhere.

Unlike many others, he landed on his feet in 1971, and started selling real estate. Stocks did little during the subsequent decade, but the price of land and buildings skyrocketed during the seventies. Ben accurately guessed that the real boom would occur in California, Arizona, Colorado, Texas, and Florida, and hence got into the game early.

There was one group he was always superb at selling to: conservative, middle-aged business people. Not all of them, of course. Principally the ones who were in a hurry to become rich. Ben could spot that inclination with an immediacy and accuracy which was uncanny. "I can tell the ones who are hungry," he said. He could indeed, and wasn't about to let any of them escape if he could possibly help it.

Getting them interested was ludicrously easy, at least for

him. After watching Ben pitch enough products at a wide variety of people, the common themes finally became apparent. At the top of the list was the promise of a combination of profits and tax benefits.

Over the years we had seen a sizable number of salespeople attempt to sell their wares. Initially, we had assumed that some individuals were simply better at selling than others, and that personal differences in this area would lead to substantial differences in income. What we weren't ready for was how much easier it was to sell certain products, as opposed to others. With the right item, almost anyone could do decently.

For instance, most of the goods consumers buy require them to spend money they will not see again. When they purchase something they think is an investment, however, they not only expect to get their money back, they anticipate making some profit, as well. When they have been led to believe that the investment is a sound one, and they also have some cash on hand with which to invest, you would think they would be ready to proceed. The sale normally should have been an easy one to conclude.

It wasn't. Salespeople struggled, often without success. We figured that investors had been burned so frequently, and had lost substantial sums in such an endless variety of ways, they had grown more conservative. It seemed reasonable to conclude that anyone who had sustained a healthy loss, as a result of having been caught up in a speculative wave which crashed jarringly on the shore, would have wanted subsequently to proceed with more caution.

No such luck. Amazingly, what investors were worried about instead were taxes. They thoroughly enjoyed sitting there and calculating (or having someone calculate for them) all the money they stood to make on their investment. But their enthusiasm was dampened drastically by the prospect not only of paying taxes on any profit they made, but also of having their normal income taxed at much higher rates. The profit they were going to earn was delicious, but unfortunately was something of a mixed blessing. In their view, they were paying a large enough portion of their income out in taxes already. Their windfall thus was going to cost them money.

TAX-FREE PROFITS

That was where Ben's talents entered the picture. Added to the enormous skills he possessed in this area was a deep desire on the part of his potential customers, both large and small, to reduce the level of taxes they paid. He had accidentally stumbled upon what is unquestionably the spot at which American investors are most vulnerable. Offering them a profit was nice. Offering them a profit *and* a way to decrease their tax bill was Nirvana. For Ben, and people like him, that is.

It was difficult for anyone to resist his sales pitch. First of all, it wasn't necessary for him to say a great deal. As soon as people realized what he was selling, their attention increased automatically. There isn't less paranoid thinking in the United States than there is in Europe, it simply involves different institutions. Whereas abroad it swirls around Government and politics, in America it attaches itself to IRS.

Rationality and reason quickly disappear here, along with the facts. The picture we found that most people have of Internal Revenue is a bit bizarre, to say the least. Instead of seeing the agency for what it is—the tax-collecting arm of the U.S. Treasury—they think it operates with total independence, completely divorced from the Government, pursuing its own ends: that is, most thought it decides what is taxable and what is not. Few seemed to realize that it is the U.S. Congress, not the IRS, which writes the Tax Code in the first place, and that Internal Revenue is simply attempting to collect taxes which are due in accordance with that code.

Everyone wants to reduce his or her tax bill, or eliminate it altogether if possible, but is afraid to openly say so. They think Big Brother is here now, and watching them. They don't want him to get angry with them, either, for what they are just as happy to state only in terms of a whisper. They are apparently unaware that IRS does not want you to pay taxes over and above what you owe. Try sending in too much money and see what happens. "I wouldn't think of it," said one. "God only knows whether I'd ever see it again." That picture of a huge, greedy, snarling—and largely invisible—monster is the one most people believe most accurate, even though current tax law in fact encourages you to take advantage of every deduction you are legitimately entitled to in order to reduce your taxes to the lowest possible level.

Strangely, Americans typically think they are "getting away with something" and "doing something wrong" even when they (or their accountant) are well within the letter of the law in minimizing the tax they have to pay. That it was being done legally did not make their discomfort or fear of retribution any the less.

Into that enormous mass of anxiety Ben strolled, with the solution everyone was secretly seeking. He never stopped reminding them they were buying more than just a highly profitable investment. There was, you see, also this marvelous, hidden aspect to the transaction (about which we'll have to talk quietly): "You can save a *lot* of money on taxes." Watching him, we often had the feeling that what he was saying at that moment was, "Hey, as a bonus, I also have here some really wonderful feelthy peektures."

Riveted to where they sat or stood, they listened intently while Ben lovingly described a deal which was going to make their hopes and dreams come true. The maintenance, tax, and interest expenses they incurred on the building were only masking the real profits they were making. "That's your cash flow," he crowed, "to do whatever you want with. Like getting another building." And in the meantime, the property could be counted upon to "keep on rising in value, 20 percent a year, year after year." He reminded them there wasn't a moment to lose: "Inflation is making your money worthless."

After his concluding comment, you could have knocked them over with a feather: "And you'll pay *less* in taxes next year. Maybe none at all."

What few of Ben's customers knew was that the properties had been marked up to a price so high it would take ten more years of high rates of inflation for them just to break even. Furthermore, although he presented himself as being merely the sales agent, some of the units he was selling were his own, having been sold to him by the developer at a reduced price, in place of a fee. Ben had more corporations through which he owned things and did business than most people have pairs of shoes.

Although he had been a millionaire in 1968, when the value of all the stocks and options he owned ballooned to almost $2 million, he had a negative net worth two years later. Having borrowed $100,000, using as collateral what had by then become wallpaper, he was forced to repay the bank loan with loans from friends and family.

Eight years of prosperous dealings in real estate had brought his net worth up to the point where he was ready, as he put it, "to see what I can really do." What he did, however, was spend too much of his money on the land on which he intended to build "an incredible shopping center, the best in the country." Rapidly escalating building costs were quickly backing him into a corner. Sensing something was amiss, one of the construction companies involved in the project slapped a lien on the property.

That was the final blow. Ben was behind in his payments at that point, but as he put it, "thought I could keep everything in the air long enough to finish it and sell it." With construction halted and the parties battling in court, Ben fell deeper in debt daily. He declared bankruptcy sixteen months later, having lost more than $1,175,000 in two years.

Don't worry, folks, he'll be back. He is studying up on solar heating. "I'm going to be an energy expert," he told us recently.

SCARING PEOPLE FOR FUN AND PROFIT

Nicky's sales pitch makes Ben's seem cautious by comparison. But the place where they differ most sharply is in what they are selling: Ben is an eternal optimist, and stridently hawks his belief that tomorrow will inevitably be better than today. Nicky, on the other hand, excitedly peddles pessimism.

There is nothing evident in his past which would have inclined him to choose so negative a set of commercial beliefs. If anything, his childhood setting was somewhat more stable and happy than Ben's. We should add, moreover, that he doesn't look the part. Middle America in dress and manner, his close-cropped hair and pleasantness are incongruous with the impending disasters he spends so much of his time describing.

If, as he says, "The economic world as we know it today is on its last legs," why is he so unfailingly polite? Watching him, you get the feeling that in an emergency, he would say, "Duck, please." He knows very well what he is doing, though. His air of respectability makes him seem like a pillar of calm in a world full of fear (which he is doing his best to magnify).

Nicky majored in history in college. The economics courses he took he found "boring beyond belief," but largely as a result of having taken them he was able after graduation to land a job at a personal financial newsletter. It was then that he first realized that a little knowledge could be made to go a very long way.

Although neither he nor most of the newsletter's subscribers were adults during the Depression, it was the one event they had to continually dredge up in their readers' minds, in order to convince people to continue reading on. The poverty and misery experienced by millions were relived in lurid terms, which made it seem as though death itself might be preferable. Far from being the end of the message, that was only the beginning: it was indeed going to recur —and soon, they predicted. But this time, thanks to their expert advice, the readers of the newsletter would be protected —while those who weren't would not be.

It was easier to arouse fear in this area than you might imagine. Most of the people we studied, for instance, had no idea of why the economic world continued to function from one day to the next. "Momentum," said one. "It wouldn't surprise me," said another, "if it all fell apart tomorrow." "I don't know what keeps it going now," said a third, and then added, "Greed?"

Most didn't understand the world's financial dealings and didn't see any reason to, either, as long as there were no major disruptions which affected their own lives. They went through each day without giving the matter much thought, and concentrated on more mundane concerns, instead.

Others, however, were scared, particularly if they had already accumulated some assets, and hence were a part of the financial world, whether they liked it or not. Their fear that they or their assets might be vulnerable to attack attached itself to thoughts of an impending economic collapse. As we were to learn, in case after case, once someone embraces such a view, once their fears have found so secure a home, they will not easily let it loose. If there is injury in the air, they would argue, they want to be prepared. In their view, it was thus imperative for them to find out everything they could about the ills they knew would soon befall them.

That is a monumentally difficult task. After all, if they are soon going to be harmed, how much time is left for them to learn all the answers? Furthermore, what information is relevant and what part is unimportant? "All of it is relevant," said one. "I want to know everything," said another. Really? When they trip, while walking down the street, and start to fall, do they want to start learning the composition of the concrete they are about to hit? In addition, how were they going to tackle—much less solve—a problem experts who were devoting their lives to it could not? Nevertheless, they were frightened. And they wanted answers.

Nicky made them feel he had the answers. At first, that

seemed an impossible feat. Surely they knew the world in which they lived was enormously more complex than he said it was and that the one-line explanations he kept repeating as if he were stoned could not possibly have captured more than a smidgen of economic reality, if that.

It was only after we'd had a chance to compare transcripts of Nicky's conversation with a number of clients over a span of years that it became clear why he and many like him are so successful. If Chicken Little tells you the sky is falling, and you believe it, that is where you are likely to look. It's not our fine-feathered fowl's fault, of course, if while you are nervously scanning the sky, you are hit by a passing car. It certainly doesn't prove that the prediction was wrong. All it means is that you probably won't be around to see whether or not it was right.

Without realizing it, Nicky had put together an extremely effective scheme for helping his customers handle the intense anxiety they were experiencing. First, he told them their fears were realistic and well founded. That, in and of itself, they were visibly comforted to hear. It's always nice to know that you are not insane. Second, he told them they were anxious only because they could see into the future—as could he—and what they saw there was indeed disturbing. A collapse was coming. Nevertheless, their ability to see it was an asset, not a liability, even if their extraordinary insight made them jumpy when they saw something ominous out there on the horizon. Third, no matter how dire the coming events would be, they had nothing to worry about, they were told, because they were going to be totally insulated from harm. In fact, they were going to profit, while others (who wouldn't listen) suffered. How? Fourth, and most brilliant of all, they were to buy gold.

Once they bought it at Chicken Little's urging, and came to believe in it, they were free. They no longer had to try to analyze an infinitely complex world full of difficult and unpredictable people and events. All they had to do was watch one little number, which would tell them everything they needed to know: the price of gold. The world had become sweetly simple, easily understandable—and safe. To know how good that can feel, at least once in your life you have to have been lost in the dark. And scared.

"How is the world situation looking today?" we asked one of his many clients. "I don't know," he replied. "Let me find out how gold is doing. You know, there are terrible times coming. You better get ready." The equanimity, the assurance and contentment with which he uttered the words, made it obvious that he, at least, felt prepared. He then launched into a brief sermon—for our good, naturally, not his ("I'm telling you this only because I like you," he said)—to the effect that those who were unprotected would pay for the fiscal sins we had all committed in the past. "Too much spending and printing too much money," he explained. "It's all going to catch up with us, *very* soon." He concluded by repeating a phrase he had heard Nicky say just a short time before: "Any moment now, the roof is going to cave in."

To be able to greet imminent disaster with such confidence, to smugly smile knowing that cataclysmic dislocations are coming, is quite a feat. Nicky had rendered his followers' world and their anxieties manageable in a single stroke, making them feel secure and protected, and had even attended to their desire to make spectacular profits. They had bought their gold. Now all they had to do was wait.

Nicky, however, had been waiting a lot longer than they, and was growing restless. He believed his own speeches, and convinced that the beginning of the end was only days away, he took a huge position in gold futures, bought on margin. "I can't lose," he said right after he had done it.

Much to his astonishment, the price of gold proceeded to plunge $50, though the economic outlook certainly hadn't brightened. He managed to lose $970,000 of the $1,063,000 he had used in the play. Ever the pessimist, he merely commented, "I should have known." His followers never heard a word about Nicky's own financial misfortune, and although almost broke, at subsequent seminars and conventions he presented the same seemingly unflappable façade he always had.

Like Ben, he too will be back. His simple device for handling anxiety may not, at first glance, appear to have the same urgent appeal that the tax breaks Ben was offering possessed. Yet, during periods of economic uncertainty, Nicky made even more per year than Ben did during the good times. And since we can rest assured there will be periods of high uncertainty in the future too, Nicky and people like him can count on finding plenty of customers who will be looking for the simple solutions he peddles.

His future followers, however, are likely to suffer the same fate his past ones did. While they were hypnotically watching the price of gold go bouncing along, they were hit, not by a passing car, but by a mass of passersby who continued doing their jobs and hence who pulled farther ahead. Had his followers simply bought gold as a hedge against soaring inflation rates, put it away and not thought about it continually, that would have been one thing. But the reverse happened. Instead of worrying less about their financial future, they began worrying more. Although they said they felt protected, they in fact increased substantially the amount of time they devoted to an obsessive concern with an impending economic collapse.

In one way, that made sense. After all, they now had an investment in a bleak outcome. They were banking on a bust. Why then should they just sit there and calmly do their jobs? Many were nervously resigned to another Depression and thus significantly reduced the pace of their normal work involvement. That's what hurt them in the long run.

We don't mean to knock any variety of investment. If it turns a profit for you, fine. But as it turns out, any investment that helps detach you from work you enjoy and makes you anxious about the future better produce a million-dollar profit, because it is costing you the best chance you have, by far, of making a fortune.

THE MAKING OF A CON ARTIST

Instead of examining the other nine examples, it is important to see what the eleven had in common.

From the speed with which their wealth grew, you may already have guessed that they did not use a slow-growth social route to accumulate their fortunes. In fact, as a group, they are characterized by a remarkably high level of animosity toward almost everyone they meet. However, they were good at keeping their blazing hostility hidden, and did socialize whenever they thought it would suit their purposes.

Primarily what they looked for from partying and public appearances was a source of new customers and high visibility. As one put it, "I'm my own best advertisement." They had no intention of walking on eggs for months and perhaps years, courting people to whom they would ultimately make a sales pitch.

Right from the start in their first encounter with someone, they either announced their line of work or, far more often, had someone else—the host or hostess—announce it proudly for them. The suckers usually took the bait themselves. They didn't have to be coaxed into buying something they wanted so badly, anyway. The questions poured out of the hungry: "How do I get in on this?", making it seem as if the salesman were being badgered during his leisure hours, forced to keep selling instead of finally having a chance to just stand around with a drink in hand and chat with old friends. Masters at making the conversation look like an imposition, they nevertheless always made certain to give the "suckers" their business card or phone number, so that the person could take the next step toward happiness.

Although each of the eleven became quite wealthy, their quest had little to do with money. Each was a High Roller, and the huge amounts which came pouring in certainly were very satisfying when they came. But of enormously greater importance to each was to "show'em." "I want *everyone* to know I'm the best," said one. "How dare he challenge me?" said a second. "No one is worth more than I am," said a third. And a fourth, "They should be paying me $1,000 a minute just to be in my presence."

The money they were able to get people to pay them was a means of getting even. It was a fee imposed upon everyone for previously ignoring them. The price they exacted was also evidence, sorely needed proof, that they were absolutely unique and unequivocally outstanding. "They are *happy* to pay me," said one in a giddy and unguarded moment, "to hear *anything* I have to say."

The five factors discussed in the previous chapter—acceptance, money, the joy of wheeling and dealing, revenge, and superiority, which serve on occasion to motivate us all—in these eleven were out of control. Even when each was well past the point of being a millionaire, none could stop. Slowing themselves down would have required them to realize, "I've made it." They could apply the brakes only after having "showed'em all" to their satisfaction.

And as far as they were concerned, that hadn't happened yet. In fact, they hadn't even come close. Hurtling forward, spending whatever came in immediately to further strengthen their ability to, as one put it, "stick it to them," they finally and inevitably overextended themselves and went bankrupt. Beginning over again meant starting from scratch. None had put any money away.

They had all learned something valuable in the process, however, and knew it. "I did it once," said one, "I'll do it again." They had developed and refined a system which gave the appearance of solving a problem we all have, in varying degree. The universal desire to reduce taxes and to stroll calmly through the threatening winds of a coming economic storm—while profiting with every step—makes us all vulnerable. The weaknesses these eleven, and the many like them, seek to exploit aren't about to disappear. And hence neither will they.

In short, an intense need for revenge and superiority turned out to be the recipe required for the making of a con artist. Since both of those needs are normal, in small amounts, each of us on occasion has the potential to do a bit of conning of our own. However, there is a compelling reason why we should make an effort to draw the bulk of our motivation to work from other sources. And these eleven make clear what the reason is: we are far too likely to be in business only briefly, in an attempt to satisfy needs which apparently no degree of success at our work can satisfy. Confronting personal problems separately, and finding work you enjoy as well, are the best revenge. And coincidentally, will maximize your chances of becoming—and staying—rich.

CHAPTER TEN

Competition

One topic which worried almost everyone we followed was how well everyone else was doing. None of us works in a vacuum. What other people are busy with can have a profound effect on how well our own efforts are received. Someone else, in fact, may already have completed the very project we were at work on, and have done it better besides.

Competition obviously plays an important part in our lives, whether we like it or not. It was a topic every multimillionaire we interviewed at the conclusion of our study had spent a great deal of time thinking about. For instance, Calvin Klein and his partner, Barry Schwartz, who together have built Calvin Klein, Ltd., from a $12,000 investment in 1968 into a business now worth over $100 million—a spectacular success story—told us:

"You can't possibly like everyone you work with in a large corporation. But if it's your own business, you can make certain that the people around you are the ones you *want* to have there.

"You can reduce the amount of friction. Some is inevitable, but you can keep it to a minimum. You have to. That is the single biggest destroyer of businesses that otherwise would have prospered. They should have: they had everything going for them. But they spent too much time fighting.

"We were determined never to compete with one another. Our business is organized so that our areas of responsibility don't even overlap. We *discuss* everything, but we never interfere with one another. When one of us makes a decision, the other goes along with it—for better or for worse. We've never regretted that."

Norman Lear had similar feelings, and told us, "The terrible thing about competing with the people around you is that it feeds on itself. It becomes hard, and sometimes impossible, to shut off. But if things are good, it shouldn't be there at all.

"When 'All in the Family' became a very successful series, a lot of press people kept asking everyone connected with the show, 'Who's responsible for its success? Bunker or Lear?' Carroll O'Connor and I never allowed that kind of thinking to interfere with what we were doing. I *knew* he was presenting a better Archie Bunker on the screen than I had put into the script. He was making an undeniable contribution, all his own."

Carroll O'Connor returned the compliment, stating that without Lear's excellent scripting of the character, "Bunker would have been just a stupid—and boring—loudmouth." Lear continued, "We needed each other. Competing with one another for who deserved *more* of the credit would have been ridiculous. When a working relationship is a good one, there is always enough credit to go around."

OVERT COMPETITIVENESS

Judged by their actions, very few of the people we studied agreed with such sentiments. To see where their competitiveness was of use, and where it proved destructive—and why—we need to examine some examples.

Beverly is one of the most competitive people we studied. A

business major in college, she found school a waste of time. "Anything I'm not getting paid for is," she added. She was open about her ambitions and saw no reason to mask them. "One day," she said, "I'm going to be *very* rich."

Her first job after college was in retailing. She was impressed by the size of the company for which she was working and the volume of merchandise it managed to move each year. Right from the start, her attitude on the job was, "Anything you can do, I can do better." Her supervisor, a woman with more than thirty years in the business, was secure enough to find the attitude charming, instead of threatening or offensive.

But there were times when Beverly's rush to display skills she hadn't yet developed brought her into direct conflict with her boss. After being with the store for a little over four years, Beverly became convinced that the merchandise in the departments which were her concern was poorly arranged. "You can never find what you're looking for on this floor," she told her boss. "We have to redo the entire floor."

What she had in mind was to rearrange their sales space so that "everything would be laid out in large circles." That way, when people were standing in the midst of one of the circles, they'd be able to see everything there in a single sweep of their gaze. Something else would be accomplished, as well: "What they'd see," she said, "would really knock them off their feet."

Her supervisor didn't appear to find such a victory over the customers' senses appealing, and instead told Beverly bluntly that the trend in retailing was in the opposite direction. "More small shops and designer corners are what we need," she said. "Our customers are too confused and overwhelmed as it is." Beverly countered, "The customers aren't getting to see even *half* the things we've got out there now." "So what?" she was told. "They're never going to, either. All that matters is that they find *some* place on the floor catchy enough to stop there and shop." She went on to explain, "There is no reason for us to parade every last piece of merchandise we have past their noses. They'd be here for a week." There the matter rested; no changes were to be made.

Nevertheless, Beverly intended to prove her point, and got the opportunity she was seeking ten months later, when her supervisor went on vacation for three weeks. By telling the three salespeople in a particular portion of the floor that she had permission, she had the merchandise in their section—white goods: sheets, towels, and pillow cases—arranged in the shape of a large oval. She found it stunning, and hoped the increased sales volume would justify leaving it that way.

Her supervisor, upon returning, found it infuriating and fired her, but not before pointing out loudly that sales in the section had decreased during the three weeks. "Nicely shaped counters don't help sell anything," she stated. "We've already tried that, and all we did was throw away over $20,000."

What made the battle between the two noteworthy was that it characterized the kinds of conflict Beverly was to continue having for the next fifteen years. In each instance, Beverly had a boss she was intent upon competing with. "I can do it better than ——," she would say with conviction. Since she deserved each person's position, she expected to be given it. "Just like that?" we asked. "Why not?" she said, annoyed. "I *am* better than they are, you know."

She had seven jobs during the twenty years and was repeatedly amazed each time she attacked someone's competence, seeking to knock them out of their spot and step into it herself, that they clung to it with such tenacity. "All they're doing is taking up space," she commented.

Joel had a similar attitude toward the people with whom he worked. He was one of four children, all boys, who were openly pitted against one another by their parents. ("Look how well your younger brother is doing," said a letter from home to Joel, while one to the younger brother stated, "If you don't try harder, you'll never be a match for your older brother.") Fortunately, the four were talented and were able to handle the pressure without obvious strain.

Joel in particular seemed to enjoy it. He candidly copied

whatever he saw people around him doing and being rewarded for. Like Beverly, he expected to be applauded at the very least, and at best, given the same pay they were getting if he could do their work better than they.

He did not spread his attempts to keep up with—and then surpass—everyone in every field. Instead, he competed primarily with people who were close to him. And the closer they were, the more intensely he found himself competing with them.

Although he majored in biology in college, he made a beeline for the business world after two years of graduate school. "Enzymes are interesting," he said, "but I don't want to be a biochemist." Four years and three jobs later he wound up working at a large metropolitan hospital.

As it turned out, someone with his interest in upstaging others could not have picked a better place to be employed. What he described as "backstabbing and buck-passing" were everywhere in the institution. "Everyone wants to be the boss," he said, "but they don't know what the hell they're doing."

The hospital had a quasi-military structure, with lines of authority clearly drawn. Yet unlike the case with a branch of the Armed Forces, the entire structure could be stood on its head if someone on the bottom discovered a mistake that someone higher up in the hierarchy had made. Instead of quietly reporting it, they usually exploited it for all it was worth. Their "lowly position," they were then quick to remind everyone, was obviously not so lowly after all.

Most of the hospital's employees seemed to bare their claws only occasionally, primarily when they felt cornered. But Joel, working in the administration office, liked to hear about other people's mistakes, and had an exceptional ability to remember them. After he had been on the job for fourteen months, Tim was hired to help handle financial relations with and disbursements from the city, state, and especially federal government. What happened next was almost predictable.

Although Joel had previously shown not the slightest interest in government funding of hospitals, he quickly moved to become an authority on the subject. The knee-jerk manner in which he responded to Tim's arrival was almost too obvious to overlook. But apparently it went unnoticed, except for Joel's suddenly increased energy, about which a few people commented. "It's the spring," he told them in reply. "I'm always this way in the spring."

It took Tim a while to realize that even though Joel was two doors away, there was no escaping him. He tried to do his work with extra care, knowing it would be scrutinized in a thoroughly critical manner. But the gap between the two was rapidly closing. It had taken Joel almost thirty months to learn the basics, but as soon as he felt comfortable enough to begin challenging Tim at meetings, he did. It took another six months for him to wear Tim's credibility down. And by the end of that year, he asked for and received permission to consolidate Tim's area of responsibility into his own, "as a cost-reducing measure," he said.

In the remaining eleven years of the twenty we've followed him, Joel continued the pattern. Tim's departing comment did, however, help make those who were staying on and who worked with Joel see him in a clearer light. "That guy is a barracuda," he said.

SECRET COMPETITORS

Although there are plenty of Beverlys and Joels, what sets them apart is the openness with which they attempt to seize victory. Most go about trying to do the same things they do, but more quietly. In fact, we found that the vast majority of competitive people are very sneaky indeed.

Gail is a teacher. Her friends think of her as hardworking and sociable. She laughs easily and often, and usually dresses casually. Bright and polite, very little about her seems out of the ordinary. But she is as competitive as anyone could possibly be—without having it show.

She has so intense a desire to at least keep up with anything achieved by those around her, it is sometimes difficult for her to sit still. When someone begins describing an accomplishment of theirs, Gail is forced to almost bite her tongue, to avoid blurting out a description of something she has accomplished which is of equal or greater merit.

It isn't something she even thinks about. It just happens. The people who are present may merely be talking about themselves, not boasting, yet it triggers in Gail an automatic and nearly uncontrollable inclination to say, "Wait. Listen to this. I've got a story that is much better than yours." But she doesn't say it. In fact, she doesn't say anything. She just listens. Tensely.

Since she doesn't openly challenge the people around her, she is forced to use a much more devious route to prevent them, in her own mind anyway, from pulling ahead of her. What she did with Brenda is typical. Once a year a national conference is held, to which both she and Brenda go. It is a chance for people in the field to get together; a few invited addresses are given, papers are read and discussed, and last but by no means least, jobs are searched for. And in Brenda's case, found. It wasn't that she wanted to leave. She knew, though, that if she got an offer from another institution, she was more likely to get the promotion she wanted at the place she now worked.

News of the success Brenda had at the convention made Gail ready for war. Guerrilla war. When the head of the department of which Gail and Brenda were members commented upon the offer, Gail quietly but quickly replied that she found it hard to see why they had made the offer at all, since Brenda had "no intention of leaving anyway and was just bucking for a promotion." Upon hearing that, the department head dropped a plan which had been hastily put together to make certain Brenda stayed. She did, but without the raise she was on the verge of being given.

The incident was representative of many which subsequently occurred. It has never been Gail's practice to say something hostile or critical directly to the people who accidentally activated her intense competitiveness. That she did behind their backs. And rather subtly, too. A look, a mild sneer, an "I'm not so sure"; "I can't imagine why," or a "They must be blind" was all it took.

One of the most skilled character assassins, she never resorted to diatribes or blistering attacks. Gail found that impossible to do in front of the person she wanted to demolish, and was almost as inhibited about doing it when the person wasn't around. Instead, to their faces, she smiled nervously. And in their absence, worked almost silently with a razor-sharp knife.

Ron, an architect intent on beating out every other architect he came in contact with, operated in a similar manner. He differed, though, in being more cordial than Gail to people whom he wanted to upstage, often questioning them at length about themselves and their work in an ever so pleasant and chatty manner. Where his way and Gail's parted company most radically was in the things he was prepared to say about his competitors behind their back. Namely, anything. Then, his hostile feelings were no longer concealed, and whether it was done quietly or loudly, calmly or savagely, he was prepared to cut someone to ribbons. The joviality he displayed when his rivals were present was matched by the ferocity he evidenced when they were not.

Curiously, most people considered him good-natured. They simply took it for granted that the amiable manner he usually displayed continued to exist after they had left. They seem not to have noticed how much of his conversation was critical of others, and that once they themselves departed, they might be the subject of similarly harsh comments made by Ron to others.

A good part of what allowed Ron to keep operating as he did was his sense of humor. Although he judged his competitors ruthlessly, he discussed any flaws he could find in a comic fashion. His audience thought he was entertaining them at someone else's expense, when in fact, he had to be entertaining in order to continue getting away with the derisive comments he constantly made.

Ron's treatment of his boss, Andy, was typical. Andy was short, fat, and bald, characteristics which Ron made certain found their way into every reference he made to Andy. The fact that Andy ran a successful and rapidly expanding architecture firm, one at which people enjoyed working, elicited a tremendous amount of antagonism from Ron. "People give him business because they feel sorry for him," Ron quipped. "He can barely see what's on the drafting tables without a stepladder."

During one of the many trips Andy took in an attempt to generate new business, Ron realized he could grab a certain portion of the firm's business for himself. It wasn't business he particularly enjoyed, but Andy liked it and was bringing in as much of it as the firm's current staff could handle. Under the guise of lending a helping hand, Ron began coordinating the incoming contracts, and in Andy's absence, parceling out the work.

Much to his chagrin, Andy then obtained a substantial contract for a cluster of apartment houses which Ron thought the firm had little chance of landing. Scurrying to shift direction and abandon his old areas of responsibility, hoping to get in on some of the new, Ron almost played his cards too openly. Sensing Ron's desperation, one of his co-workers said to him, "Why don't you stop trying to outshine Andy?"

Ron was rattled by the remark, but managed to recover with sufficient speed to be able to reply, "He needs some assistance, and I'm just trying to give it to him. That's all." But Andy didn't want any from Ron on this particular project, the largest design contract the firm had ever received. Instead, he told Ron to continue on with what he was doing.

Ron has, but for six years he has also been making plans to leave with as much of that business as he can, and either take it to another firm or use it to start one of his own.

VICIOUS COMPETITORS

It would be easy to conclude from the examples cited thus far that there are only two types of competitive people. Those who compete openly, such as Beverly and Joel. And those who are secret competitors, such as Gail and Ron.

However, not everyone who is competitive fits neatly into one of the two categories. In fact, there are a large number of people who are both: openly competitive *and* secretly so, as well. After encountering even a few of them, the words and actions of more normally competitive individuals begin to seem mild by comparison.

Elizabeth doesn't appear at first glance to be making much of an effort to mask her desire to compete with those around her. Almost any challenge she is offered she will attempt to meet. When someone in her office mentions that they are good at something, Elizabeth either tells them that she too is or else finds something else to present at which she is equally good.

The degree of discomfort she experiences when someone goes so far as to brag is sizable. And in such instances, she does what many intensely competitive people do. Rather than attempting to match the person, step for step, she attacks them. Becoming openly abusive, she tries to quiet the boasting in order to quiet herself. She often comments, "My nerves are shot," after such outright conflict. But interestingly, they are no less shot when she can't shut the person up and has to sit there and listen to people praise themselves, however briefly.

Her explosive reaction to what she sees as other people's attempts to provoke her are exhausting. In the course of a normal day, many little self-congratulatory comments are casually dropped by the people with whom she works. And reacting strongly to each, by day's end the cumulative effect is enormous, and debilitating.

In spite of the considerable quantity of animosity she evidences when there is a contender around, most of her competitive feelings surface only when the person who stimulated them is absent. For instance, she, Renée, and Lisa have worked together for almost four years, selling an expensive apparel line primarily to large department stores. Although each of the three has been given a separate list of accounts to service, in order to prevent them from stepping on one another's toes, it is common for them to talk to one another's customers. If Renée is out for the day, Elizabeth routinely handles the visit or call. Or if two buyers come to see Elizabeth at the same time, Renée would ordinarily assist, if she isn't busy.

There is good reason for them to work together, since besides their salary, a large portion of their pay comes to them as commissions based on the aggregated volume of apparel sold. The pooling arrangement is supposed to guarantee that each of the three has a strong interest in the total sales effort.

Everyone who works with Elizabeth knows how aggressive she is. Even so, they would be amazed to learn of the lengths to which she is prepared to go to make certain she alone gets the credit for any major sales which are made. When Elizabeth ran into the President of the firm, she commented in passing that Renée hadn't been doing well with the buyer from Saks—until Elizabeth quietly held up an item "that really got them interested." Renée, she acknowledged, would have gotten around to showing it sooner or later, "but by then the buyer would have been asleep." Elizabeth went on to say that Renée hadn't even seen her hold the garment up, nor was she going to tell her. "I'm not looking for the credit," she said. "I just want to help."

On another occasion, Lisa made a substantial sale. It took Elizabeth completely by surprise, since the accounts Lisa had were not as large as the ones she and Renée serviced. It was going to be a great day for Lisa, because no sooner had she finished writing up the order than another of her good customers arrived. Elizabeth offered to run the paper work already completed over to the billing and accounting office, the next step in the processing of a purchase order. Lisa said, "Fine."

On the way down the hall, Elizabeth stopped in an empty office, quickly rewrote the order in her own handwriting, and then signed it, making it seem as if she had been the one who supervised the sale. Passing the office of the Vice-President in charge of merchandising, she stopped in briefly, proudly flashed the order, and then proceeded on her way.

It had been a risky thing to do, because in destroying the old slip and writing a new one, it had become necessary for her to forge the buyer's signature. She wasn't worried about it, though, since the order would soon be punched into a machine, while the slip of paper—now no longer important—would be filed away.

Leon's behavior was similar. Tall and lean, with a scholar's appearance, he gazed tiredly at people through wire-rimmed glasses which made him seem somewhat slow-moving and resigned. When it came to bump competitors out of the picture, however, he had a limitless amount of energy.

Alex was closest to him in terms of their respective areas of responsibility, as well as their positions on the corporate ladder. And while anyone who got near Leon could sooner or later count on feeling his sting, most of his venom was currently being aimed in Alex's direction. At meetings, Leon would sit quietly and wait for a good opportunity to make Alex look like a bumbler.

In a transformation which turned Leon from an old schoolteacher into a poisonous snake in a matter of seconds, he would lash out at what he called an idiotic action or remark on Alex's part, and then immediately become composed once again. Instead of making his own behavior seem absurdly inconsistent, he made it appear he had spoken up only because he had been confronted by an imbecility so outrageous it warranted the outburst.

Next to Alex his closest competitor was Randy, with whom he was supposed to be coordinating his efforts. Randy had worked all week, and weekend, on a marketing plan which he showed to Leon on Monday morning. Leon was shaken by what he read. He realized that the information contained in the report was both insightful and useful, and it made no mention of him. He pretended he hadn't studied it—in fact, hadn't even had a chance to look at it—and got Randy's permission to take it home that evening and read it.

Making certain that it never returned cost Leon the use of his favorite attaché case, which he claimed had been stolen with the report in it. It and the report are sitting in a closet at home, but to Leon it was worth it. He had the only copy and knew there was no way for Randy to rewrite the report in time for the monthly meeting on Wednesday, at which he wanted to present it. By the time of the next meeting, Leon knew he would already have had a chance to discuss the ideas with the others, as if he had come up with them on his own.

Since Leon claimed he had never even had a chance to look at it, whenever Randy publicly lamented what a loss the disappearance of his report was, Leon could humor him, replying offhandedly, "I'm sure it was good," and then adding, "but that case of mine was irreplaceable."

INITIAL VICTORIES

Elizabeth and Leon are two of the most maliciously competitive people in positions of power we studied. They are willing to lie, cheat, and steal—and often do—if that will help them eliminate a rival. However, the key question is: How successful were they?—and we don't mean as just exterminators of other people's dreams, but in furthering their own goals.

The answer turned out to be simple, but bewildering: the more intensely competitive someone was, the *less* likely they were to become wealthy. The first few cases in which that conclusion began to become apparent were, we thought, exceptions to the rule. At the beginning of this study, we fully expected to see the most competitive people emerge two decades later as the most successful by far.

And initially, at least, our expectations weren't disappointed. In a substantial number of instances, extremely competitive people managed to bump their rivals out of the picture and move ahead more quickly as a result. As veteran competitors they had learned a wide variety of techniques over the years which could be used to make someone else seem inadequate.

They were often the first to be promoted. Elizabeth, for example, beat out Renée and Lisa for the position of sales manager. When we asked her boss, "What made you choose Elizabeth?" the reply was immediate: "She's a real go-getter." Similarly, Leon won out over Alex and two others for the position of marketing director. The reason again was simple: "He makes fewer mistakes than the others. Not as spastic."

When an assistant department head was chosen, it turned out to be Gail, not Brenda. "Brenda," the department head said, "plays politics." Similarly, after Joel got Tim fired and made someone else on the staff seem incompetent by comparison, Joel was later placed in charge of financial planning for the hospital. His supervisor admiringly stated at the time, "He makes the others look bad."

He does indeed. In fact, he, Beverly, Ron, Gail, Leon, and Elizabeth appear to know just about every trick in the book for accomplishing that purpose. Yet, as well armed as these six and the many like them were, their initial victories were—amazingly—not followed by subsequent successes. It was striking to see that, in case after case, although they had started out very well and were ahead at the middle of the twenty-year race, they were well behind at the finish.

Something major was happening along the way. It became crucial to identify the specific factors and the precise point at which the advancement process in each case began breaking down.

Elizabeth, for example, had no trouble grabbing credit from Renée and Lisa for sales she hadn't made. Far more skilled than they at making others seem worthless and herself flawless, she was able to convince her superiors she was the one who deserved to be promoted.

They agreed, until they got to know her better. As a result of her promotion, she was brought into closer contact with them. It was only then that things changed. They hadn't known about the maneuvers she had successfully used against Renée and Lisa. But when they themselves were exposed to similar treatment, they were shocked.

Her two immediate superiors, Trudy and Martin, decided to propose that a new division be opened, supplying a higher-priced line, for which they felt there was now a market. They had been mulling it over for months, and after working out a preliminary budget and sales plan, and assessing the need for additional space and personnel, were ready to present the plan to Jack, the firm's President.

Although they had kept their thoughts about a new division to themselves while they researched and reconsidered the alternatives, once the plan was ready they mentioned it to their co-workers, including Elizabeth. She responded by saying, "It *is* a good idea." When the plan was presented and Elizabeth heard that it had been favorably received, she wasted no time. Seeing Jack in the hallway, she mentioned that, "I *told* them it was a good idea," leaving the unmistakable impression that she, not they, had originated it.

Jack in turn mentioned her comment to them a few days later, and they were incensed. "I was livid," said Trudy. "We worked *really* hard on that plan." They said nothing to her. But they were extremely aware of every similar comment Elizabeth made from then on. For the last six years, she has received no promotions. Nor will she. Why do they keep her at all? "She's a good saleswoman," Martin said. Why doesn't she leave? "I'll be damned if I'd tell my friends [at other companies] anything good about her," said Trudy.

Joel, too, found himself running into increasing resistance as the race progressed. Having been promoted, Joel assumed that, as he put it, "From here on, it'll be easy." It wasn't. Just as in Elizabeth's case, he continued using the same tactics he had employed all along. Indeed, there was no reason for him not to. As far as he could see, they had worked rather well.

But when the hospital's top management decided to switch to a decentralized system of financial administration, so as to keep better track of divisional expenses, Joel balked. What bothered him was that he hadn't proposed the idea, and in fact, hadn't even thought of it. The credit, and more importantly the responsibility, for administering the new system was going to be in the hands of Joel's chief rivals in the accounting office.

Using a traditional technique, he moved to discredit the three people principally involved in promoting the new system. This time, though, things were different. Tim had been easy to defeat. This trio proved another matter entirely, and refused to even fight about it. They simply pointed out how much more information it would provide and hence how easy it would be to economize wisely, where necessary. "It offers greater understanding," said one of the three, "and control."

Joel moved to accomplish from within what he was unable to do as an outsider. He tried befriending one of the three who seemed accessible, by inviting the person to play tennis with him. Tim's farewell blast hadn't been forgotten, however, and aware of what Joel was up to, he was rebuffed. Within seven months of the implementation of the new system, Joel's area of responsibility had shrunk by almost half. During that time, Joel's every tactic appeared. "I think I know him better now," said his supervisor grimly, at the end of the period.

What worked for Elizabeth, Joel, and others like them in the early part of the race increasingly began to backfire badly as the years passed. Had they been able to control their intensely competitive feelings, the outcome would have been different over the years. But they couldn't. And the higher in their field they rose, the more self-destructive their competitiveness became.

A HUMILIATING LOSS

Why couldn't they stop? What drove them to undo many years of hard work?

What *is* the competitor's nightmare? In short, it is a fear of losing. They hate to lose. Hate it so much the very prospect of it makes them furious, and to some extent berserk. Their mind races and they run off automatically in all directions at once, in a frenzy. Don't let them kid you: winning doesn't count, or even register in their mind. All that really matters is avoiding a loss.

Unfortunately for them, the higher they rose in their field, the more they had to lose. "I'm the marketing VP," said Leon, mortified, "I *should* have known that," about a sales figure someone else had cited at a meeting. "Why wasn't I told?" said Elizabeth, horrified at the news that Lisa had made yet another large sale and this time proudly announced it herself. "I have to be told *first*. *I'm* the sales manager."

Instead of attaining an expanding sense of accomplishment and security, their position was becoming increasingly fragile. The stakes were smaller in the early part of the race, when all the runners were bunched together anonymously. But they were spread out now. And each had to publicly fight the others for position, alone. Losing was going to be humiliating. Anything which prevented it from happening was acceptable.

"THE OLDEST ESTABLISHED PERMANENTLY SHIFTING ALLIANCES IN THE WORLD"

The majority of competitive people we studied tried to be sneaky about it. They wanted their intensely competitive feelings to remain a secret. Yet even in instances where they succeeded in hiding them from everyone, including themselves, the very presence of those feelings turned out to be very costly, for three reasons.

First, competitive people generated a great deal of divisiveness. No matter how harmoniously a group may have been functioning, once someone who was extremely competitive joined it the harmony disappeared. Significant degenerative changes occurred in every work or social circle of which they became a member. Without realizing why, everyone suddenly felt an increased need to "uphold my end," "keep up," and "defend myself." They may not have known specifically how and when they were being attacked and challenged, but they knew it was happening, nonetheless.

Dividing the group up into isolated individuals makes a competitive person's life easier. Elizabeth knew how to separately handle Lisa and Renée. Yet she found them menacing as a team and moved to do anything and everything necessary to split them up, including having Lisa's desk moved to the other end of the showroom in which the three spent the bulk of their day. Leon similarly did whatever he could to foster hostility and distance between Randy and Alex.

Not one of the competitive people we studied was aware of the disagreement and ill will they constantly sought to stir up around them. But above all, they wanted to avoid losing. And they knew that two (or more)-against-one was more likely to result in a loss than one-against-one. To make certain they weren't the one everyone else might gang up on, they felt compelled to fragment every group.

They also went a step further, and pretended to team up with everyone against everyone else. Instead of being on the outside, they always tried to be on the inside, the winning side. They were always your ally against your enemies (even if they had to make some for you, so you'd need an ally)— and then shifted alliances in a flash and became an ally to your enemies when you were out of the room.

A key question is: Why was the divisiveness competitive people caused so costly to them? Why did it ultimately prevent them from receiving any further promotions or offers?

The answer is that the higher you rise in a corporate or institutional setting, the more important a part of your job it is to maintain a "happy family" atmosphere among your coworkers. The people occupying the lower slots won't do it, and aren't expected to, either. Moreover, it is an addition to, not a substitute for, your other duties. Most of your associates would be suspicious of your saying, "Let's hear it for the company," and, "Three cheers for the firm." But the goal can be achieved in a different, less offensive manner. Without question, those who did it best were those who merely concentrated on doing a good job.

However, that was never the first priority of competitive people, and slowly but surely it became apparent. "I won't move her up," said Trudy about Elizabeth, "because she'd have us at one another's throats." Similarly, Leon's boss said of him that "he makes a lot of unnecessary enemies." Gail was said to "pit people against one another," and Joel was adjudged "hardworking, but a troublemaker."

It is a subtle but important point. Your employer isn't going to tell you to foster a spirit of cooperation in those around you. It is simply assumed of you, if you are to be promoted repeatedly. And if it's not there, neither will the promotions be. Nor can it be faked; we've all gotten good at sensing the phony cheerleading of intensely competitive people who merely want the credit for "making everyone pull together."

When all is said and done, competitive people did not compete very well over the years with those who enjoyed their field. In fact, it wasn't even a contest. Those who were absorbed by their work had accidentally gotten their own egos out of the picture, thus making it easier for them get their co-workers' egos out of the picture and hence reduce divisiveness to an absolute minimum. They unwittingly generated more harmony and cohesion, and in the later stages of the race to riches that feature became increasingly important.

The second reason competitiveness turned out to be so costly is that it is "small-minded." That is not how it's usually thought of, but that is how it actually evidenced itself. The focus was on keeping up with, or beating, someone else. And it turned out to be too local a focus.

The third reason competitiveness ultimately prevented wealth was that it is too stop-and-go. Nothing energized competitive people more than having someone to compete with. Unfortunately, when there was no one around to compete with, their energy and interest decreased.

That happened in hundreds of instances. It was amazing to see someone who had cursed and sabotaged a competitor fall apart when the person left to go elsewhere. Joel floundered without direction for weeks after Tim left. If Leon didn't know what Randy and Alex were up to, he didn't know what he himself was supposed to be up to. When Elizabeth had to run the showroom herself for a while, at first she was elated, thinking that all the credit would of necessity be hers. But then, having congratulated herself on her wonderful position, she quickly began to lose interest in the whole business. "I hate them," she said, "but I guess I need them."

The local and the stop-and-start nature of competitiveness combined too easily. When there was no one around to compete with, some stopped working altogether and merely went through the motions until a new source of fear arrived on the scene. That proved very damaging in the long run, since it resulted in their being pulled first in one direction, then another, and then a third, depending upon who was around at the time. To even discuss persistence under such circumstances is a joke.

Even if the people to be copied were famous, their eminence and the achievements on which it was based are yesterday's news. And your own fame and fortune will have to be based on tomorrow's. The only way anyone we studied became part of the future was to persist. Everyone who copied was, at best, attempting to merely redo someone else's past.

It is now clear that you can "scratch and claw" your way up, all right—to the middle-level positions. No higher. In spite of the frequency with which we heard people describe the supposedly vicious competitiveness required to "get you to the top," it turns out that it will get you only to the middle. And much to the surprise of people who operate in this manner, there they will find lots of others as competitive as they, all ready and waiting.

In fact, we were amazed to discover that there is a Middle Management Asteroid Belt. If you hope to one day become wealthy, you cannot avoid passing through it. It is a zone consisting of extremely competitive people whose careers have come to a halt.

No matter how absorbing you find your work, you can expect to encounter a fair amount of malicious and sneaky competitiveness in the Asteroid Belt. And that will be the case even if you are self-employed or free-lance. The fact that you are not a full-time employee of the firm for which they work will not make them see you as any less of a threat.

For instance, the reception given outside suppliers by Elizabeth and Leon, on the one hand, and Trudy and Randy, on the other, are typical. And remarkably different. Elizabeth hung up on someone who wanted to show her some new cases and racks which would display the merchandise she was selling more attractively. Yet when the person got in touch with Trudy, he was struck by the contrast between the two. Busy as she was, Trudy found ten minutes to look at the new structures.

No sale resulted. But as the salesman put it, "That's OK. I don't expect to make a sale every time." And then, referring to Elizabeth, he added, "But that other one is just vicious." Similarly, an outside supplier who talked to both Leon and Randy commented, "It's hard to believe those two work for the same firm." They do, but Randy and Trudy keep moving up. Leon and Elizabeth haven't been, and aren't likely to.

On the other side of the Asteroid Belt, the atmosphere usually changed drastically. Those at the top were absorbed by their work far more than were those in the middle, and that is what allowed them to get to the top in the first place.

We found only one, very disturbing exception to that general conclusion. Some top executives didn't get there because they loved the company's area of business, accidentally persisted, and ultimately rose to the top. Instead, they were simply given the top slot by their parents.

THE CONSEQUENCES OF INFERIORITY

The typical situation was one in which the father started the business, expanded it considerably, and during the later years slowly transferred his stock in the company into his children's hands. While that should have guaranteed the prevalence of harmony and continuity, the reverse was so. We found that the companies run by executives who inherited their position were characterized by the highest level of destructive competition among its top management. In such companies, passing through the Middle Management Asteroid Belt did not allow you to enter a zone of genuinely involved top people. Quite the contrary, there was no difference between middle and top. Rising did not cause the amount of malicious competitiveness to decrease.

How come? Here the psychological aspects of the problem became crucial. Whether consciously or unconsciously, the father had somehow succeeded in seriously harming his children's sense of adequacy. Let us assume for the moment that no parent would deliberately do such a thing, and that the damage was inflicted unwittingly. That could easily happen. These, after all, were largely self-made men, and the drive and ambition they possessed made it difficult even for their peers to match them. It is hardly surprising that their children, arriving on the scene a generation late and entering a profitable business someone else had built, felt outclassed.

But there was more. A substantial amount of bullying was aimed at the children. Put-downs were common. The old rationale was, as one put it, "It toughens them. This is a hard business." That sounds absurd to us now. Yet at one time it was assumed, at least by this group of parents, that the world is going to "box your kids' ears," as one said, "so you might as well get'em ready for what's coming by doing it to them first."

For all their good intentions, however, the results were a solid sense of inferiority in children who now run the family business. They inherited anywhere from 100 percent down to 4.2 percent of the outstanding stock, with the public usually the owners of the rest. But it was a large enough percentage to allow at least one of the children to be a principal figure in the company's planning and hiring decisions.

The person he chose as the company's top executive was rarely the one most qualified for the job, either in terms of ability, personality, or interest. Instead, what the person had to be was no threat. Remember, most intensely competitive behavior is generated by an extreme fear of losing, an outcome which is viewed as humiliating, since it allegedly provides proof at last of inferiority.

People who inherited a business weren't about to lose—repeatedly—to someone they themselves appointed to run the family firm. "He's OK," said one owner. "I can handle him." Strange criterion for a company President to meet. Often, though, they kept the top slot for themselves, and the person they hired filled the next slot down.

But how do you go about finding someone capable enough to run the firm, on the one hand, and yet who can be "handled," on the other? The search for "the manageable manager" will bring you back to the same point every time: someone who is intensely (but for the most part secretly) competitive.

Why? Two guidelines dominate such a person's actions. The first is: "Divide, and avoid being conquered." The second is: "Side with everyone against everyone else, but always be on the winning side." Anyone who has been permanently shifting alliances for any extended period knows that it may at times require some ass-kissing. You may have to "get in good" with someone, and quickly, at that. "Buttering up" the person is usually an effective way to speed up the process. It doesn't matter that you hate them; for the moment, they have the power. And that's all that counts.

The skill with which some of the people we studied apply the guidelines is immense. You have never had a friend shower you with as much warmth and companionship as they do. Attentive even when tired, willing to laugh at any lame line you might utter, they can quickly convince you that their admiration for you is unquestionably real.

And since they know that wearing a constantly smiling face would soon make you suspicious, they are even ready to disagree with you. Indeed, they may have to go so far as to argue with you, before giving in only reluctantly, of course. A show of standing their ground (about an insignificant matter) may even convince you that they are stubborn and strongminded, and hence wouldn't say or do anything they didn't honestly believe in. They are happy to let you think you are winning, because they secretly know they themselves are.

And whom do you imagine such a person chooses, in turn, as his subordinates? Competent, secure, and capable people? Ones who might wind up challenging their boss unwittingly, thanks to the quality of their work, their involvement in it, and the high performance standards they can't help but try to maintain?

Obviously not. They choose people as competitive and insecure as themselves, rather than risk losing publicly, and repeatedly, to an underling. And so it goes, layer after sick layer.

There are many such second- and third-generation family firms, and as a result, you may find yourself employed at or doing business with. In that case you may, without realizing it, be right in the midst of a thicket of shifting alliances and malicious competitors. Perhaps you already realize it, but are optimistic that the situation will soon change.

It won't. We were unable to find even one company where the chronic insecurity, and the destructive behavior it bred within the firm, evaporated. It certainly wasn't present in every family firm, but at those in which it was, it stayed. Firing people in the middle- and upper-level slots changed nothing. It was a common ritual, however.

Periodically someone would be chosen as a scapegoat. The sacrificial lambs were rarely faultless, and had some personal problems or minor incompetencies (which allowed them to obtain their job in the first place). But *everything* which seemed to be going wrong with the firm at the time was blamed on them. Once the beasts of burden left, carrying away the responsibility for last season's mistakes, the atmosphere lightened temporarily. Everyone could be friends for a while. And then, next season arrived. Unless it happened to be an outstanding one, the process began again.

The fears of the person at the top were transmitted down through the upper layers and then institutionalized, thanks to a succession of hand-picked people who were viciously (but secretly) competitive. Change, if it were ever to come, would have to begin at the top and result in the replacement of a number of key executives. Sooner or later the optimism of many of the people we studied who hoped to do well was crushed by the realization that the owners of the firm weren't about to fire themselves, and that even if they did, their carefully selected successors would remain.

It was very revealing to see what happened when the children or grandchildren of the founder of the firm decided to make themselves absentee owners. Busying themselves with hobbies and activities they enjoyed, and which their wealth allowed them to pursue at their own pace, they frequently turned their business over to professional managers, capable and talented people who would not have accepted the position in the first place unless autonomy had been assured.

"Ass-kissing didn't get me my job," said one candidly, "and it wouldn't help me keep it either, if I stopped doing what I was hired to do: make this company grow and be profitable." He has little to worry about. He is so interested in his work, he'd almost certainly have been a success at a competing firm. That would have made him a serious threat to the previously stagnant firm he is now running.

Needless to say, the difficulties created by inferiority feelings in top management were also found in a wide variety of firms that were not family owned. People who started their own company were often just as unbearable to work for as those who inherited theirs. Even if they'd wanted to, such people couldn't have held a job at a large firm for long. They had no choice but to be in business for themselves. Many employees at such firms who were deeply interested in their work, who did it well and who rose as a result, eventually encountered a top layer of executives whose personal problems caused them to overlook quality and profitability and concentrate instead on the more immediate matter of self-protection. A switch to another firm was usually called for by those who enjoyed their work.

QUIETLY UP THE LADDER

Archie McCardell, formerly the President of Xerox and now the President and Chief Executive Officer of International Harvester, a $7 billion company employing almost 96,000 people, told us:

"Over a period of time, the people I've seen become successful just concentrated on doing a good job, were modestly proud of what they were doing, and accepted compliments, when offered, but didn't *press* for recognition. I myself try to evaluate people on the basis of what they do, not say. I'm favorably impressed by people who do a good job in a quiet manner, without stepping on somebody else.

"There are some bosses who are sufficiently insecure that they need the boost that comes from having people play up to them. But the people doing the buttering up are not the ones who are going to rise in organization. They're the ones we try to avoid.

"People who compete unfairly may be able to take the first few steps up the ladder, but that's primarily because they're dealing with managers who are themselves fairly young, and perhaps playing the same games. When you get up into senior management, that's not going to work.

"In my company, that's one of the most deadly sins. I recently had to deal with a couple of people who were very competitive—and who were both very capable. But we couldn't get them to stop competing and just concentrate on doing a good job. We finally got rid of both of them.

"Unduly competitive people should be weeded out, and in fact, by the time you get up to the upper management levels the proportion of those people has become much smaller than at the lower levels. The weeding process has been at work all along, even if the process isn't perfect, or ever complete.

"Trying to take credit for something somebody else did is very common. It's also *obvious*—and it doesn't help. That doesn't mean you won't succeed by doing it, but the success rate is a lot lower than it is for people who simply do well the things they're supposed to."

Those who've worked with McCardell told us that he means what he says. As one put it, "I think Archie has succeeded *because* he lived by those words." There are many people in our sample, however, who don't share McCardell's view and who claimed that someone living by that philosophy would never do well financially. But the fact remains that in 1978 McCardell was the seventh most highly paid corporate executive in the United States, and earned $1,906,658. Two people in top management at another firm producing a similar product line, who had watched how McCardell worked and what he accomplished, said that as far as they were concerned, he was worth twice what he was being paid.

In sum, it doesn't make any difference whether your goal is to "show'em" or "beat'em." The first is revenge and the second is competition, but over the long run both proved equally unproductive for the people in our sample. Neither getting even nor keeping up turned out to be a worthwhile personal strategy. Because they both require you to live your life on other people's terms, and as it turns out, you can become rich only on your own.

CHAPTER ELEVEN

The Most Common
and Costly
Investment Mistakes

Having looked at the detours people usually took in Stage One, we come to the detours made in Stage Two. This is an important topic, affecting two large groups.

The first consists of those people who, according to our results, should have been concentrating on Stage One activities if they really wanted to become rich. Impatience or a growing indifference toward their work, however, caused them to leap ahead, hoping to become wealthy. After that, they said, they were going to turn their attention to finding an absorbing activity with which to fill their days.

The second group consists of people who had indeed been doing work they enjoyed, and who had been accidentally investing in themselves for years, but who finally had more money than they could use for that purpose.

Happily for us—though not for them—the two groups did not differ when it came to costly mistakes in investing. We won't have to separately examine the blunders each group made: both took the same detours.

What were they? And why were they taken?

MAKING AN INVESTMENT

The most common mistake investors of every description made was their decision to spend their money on things which had already been classified as investments. That sounds strange, and the best way to see what typically occurred is to compare two people, one of whom became wealthy, the other of whom did not.

Carl is a bottles freak, and has been so for every year of the two decades we've followed his activities. "There's a lot of history in old glass," he said nineteen years ago, when most people considered the stuff he was avidly collecting to be merely junk. That didn't deter him, though, and in fact, he often laughed at the many snide lines which came his way—for example, that if he continued tying up all his money in old glass, and then there were an earthquake, he and his fortune would go to pieces.

Over a twenty-six-year span, Carl has spent a fair amount on his hobby, and even finished half a manuscript on the subject, which sooner or later he'd like to complete and have published. But the bottles, not the book, always came first. Had he put the money he spent in a savings account at 5 percent per annum, compounded quarterly, he'd now have a total of $59,371, assuming the taxes due each year on the interest earned had been paid from another source.

By contrast, he was recently offered a total of $550,000 by four collectors, each of whom wanted only part of his diversified collection of old tables, windows, doors, dishes, lamps, and bottles.

Irwin, on the other hand, heard that diamonds were a good investment and started collecting them. "They're a good hedge against inflation, too," he said, "and there's always a market for them." Like Carl, though, he never really bothered testing what that market would be willing to pay for his collection. Affable and easygoing, Irwin found great comfort in the slowly rising prices he had to pay for new acquisitions.

He reasoned thusly: "I'm paying 40 percent more now for the same diamonds I bought three years ago. That has to mean the ones I have have gone up in value by 40 percent." The logic of Irwin's argument seemed impeccable—that is, until he tried to dispose of the gems and buy some building plots a friend had told him were "a foolproof investment."

Over a twenty-one-year period he had spent $71,100 on the diamonds in his collection. If each time he had bought a gem he had instead put the money in a savings account and it then started earning interest (computed as in Carl's case), Irwin would now have had $113,618. However, much to his surprise, the best offer he could get from a diamond dealer for the collection was $52,000. "But that's $19,000 *less* than I paid!" he protested. "How can that be?" The dealer's answer was stunningly simple: "I have to make a living, too, you know."

Hundreds of examples such as these were seen, but what underlies them all is this: the word "investment" is used daily by millions of people who have never stopped to consider what it means. No object is inherently an investment. It has to first make a transition from being a *thing* to being a thing which is increasing in value. After all, if it is not expected to rise in price in the next ten or twenty years, it's not much of an investment.

And second, there have to be a large and (one hopes) increasing number of people interested in it. If everyone who wants something already has it, it won't qualify as an investment. Needless to say, the two aspects of an investment—its increasing value and the increasing number of people who want it—feed on one another.

The reclassification of an object in the public's mind from "thing" to "investment" is done quietly, but it is quite a formal matter. Moreover, it always happens very quickly. A particular item—such as comic books—may go for decades without being considered of any value whatever. And then suddenly, in a mere matter of months or even weeks, crazed collectors looking for huge and instant profits will descend upon the item and reclassify it, elevating it overnight to the status of an investment.

The fact that something is scarce is what allows it to have value. As Irwin put it, "I try to collect rare things, because then I know they'll always be worth plenty." But as reasonable as that sounds it is frequently false. There are many scarce items no one wants—for example, two pieces of a broken window, one the shape of the state of Alaska, the other that of the Statue of Liberty. Obviously, what is essential is that people—lots of people—want it.

Everyone we studied realized how important it was that there be only a few of something if it were ever to become valuable. They all correctly guessed that if there were only two of a particular stamp left and then 700,000 more were found in an old trunk somewhere, the value of the two would plummet.

THE IMPRESSION OF SCARCITY

What few seemed to realize, and hence fell victim to repeatedly, is that it's remarkably easy for someone attempting to sell you something to create an impression of scarcity. How rare is the object? The fact remains that, in most instances, it's not easy to find out. Unfortunately, most people never even try to, but even if they did, the going would be rough: estimates, data, and opinions differ, and old trunks do indeed turn up.

Mark and Phyllis decided to take a trip to South America for their fifteenth wedding anniversary. Ecuador and Colombia were the two countries in which they spent most of the three weeks they were gone. While traveling in and around Quito, the capital of Ecuador, they stopped at a rustic-looking jewelry shop. Handmade rings and necklaces were what they were after. And once inside, they found an abundance of glittering gold and silver trinkets, "just what we were looking for," said Phyllis. "Quality stuff," added Mark, "and definitely not made by a machine."

One piece particularly caught their eye. A bracelet of pure gold, weighing almost a pound. "It was sensational," said Mark, "a copy of something a thousand years old, but even better than the original." The price was $2,100. "We knew the gold alone was worth a fortune," said Phyllis, "and the craftsmanship was priceless." Having learned quickly to bargain in a land where the price of everything is negotiable, they offered $1,500. The owner flatly said, "No." Besides, he reminded them, of one thing they could be certain: "There is only one." Their resistance wilted upon hearing that. "He *had* to be right," said Phyllis. "No two artists could have made it so intricate in the same way." After much haggling, they and the owner settled upon a price of $1,800. Rounding up all their cash, and obtaining more from home, they concluded the purchase.

You've probably already guessed the ending. They had been home for about seven months when a friend of theirs came to dinner with her new boyfriend. He happened to be a jeweler, and when Phyllis laughingly showed him the bracelet, saying, "It's fabulous, but it's too heavy to wear," he told them he'd recently seen two just like it. That made Mark suspicious. When they subsequently had the bracelet carefully examined, it came back with a tag, "Estimated value: $65."

Tales of tourists being hoodwinked abound, and almost no one is surprised at yet another one. Items which seemed a bargain abroad often fell apart upon arrival home or had been available more cheaply all along at a local department store.

What is amazing, however, is the frequency with which such episodes occur. All told, we recorded thousands of them —that is, each of the people we studied was buffaloed into buying something worthless or overpriced, costing $50 or more, an average of once every twenty-six months. We've all become critical shoppers, used to being bombarded by (and laughing off) a constant shower of ads. Even so, the knowledge that "there is only one left" (and we should have it!) is apparently too powerful for us to resist. Sooner or later, if not with one item then with another, we are suckered by it.

The sales pitch was different each time, yet what almost all the transactions had in common was that the seller had succeeded in creating in the buyer's mind (or the buyers themselves created) a false impression of scarcity. It doesn't make sense that we fall prey so easily to lines such as: "only a few left"; "unique"; "never have another opportunity like this again," and, "one of a kind." It may not make sense, but we do it, anyway. Who knows? Maybe the tendency, destructive though it is in an age of plenty, helped keep us alive in an age of real scarcity.

What relevance does any of this have to investing? An enormous amount. One of the fundamental aspects of every investment concerns its scarcity. And we clearly tend to exaggerate to ourselves the rarity of any object in which we become interested. As Phyllis put it, "We *had* to grab it. We knew we'd never have another chance." Our bias toward viewing things as being much rarer than they actually are would, in and of itself, make it hard for us to decide what is— or is not—an investment. But there is another significant, complicating factor: the Stage Two-first orientation of the large majority.

People who want above all to become rich want it to happen soon. When we asked them, "When would you like to be wealthy?" one replied, "Would ten minutes from now be all right? On second thought, make that five." They don't have time to carefully consider what the word "investment" means. "I don't care *what* it's called," said Irwin, "as long as it makes me rich."

In short, the tendency we all have to think of the things we want as being rare is a powder keg. A Stage Two-first orientation is a burning match. Mixing the two can be counted upon to produce an explosion. The sentence summarizing the first tendency is simple enough: "This is the only one; I've *got* to have it." So is the sentence summarizing the second: "I'm *certain* it'll make me rich." The two combine ever so easily to produce a lethal sentence: "This is the only way I can become rich."

Although they started out as two separate thoughts, occurring simultaneously in our minds, they quickly and quietly blend to form one familiar, but fatal thought: "This is my only chance. I've got to take it."

SPENDING AND SAVING

That thought is applied everywhere; not just to gems, but to jobs.

Jennifer loathed hers. The work itself was all right, but her bosses never let her do it. Constantly interfering, burdening her time with useless meetings and the writing of reports no one ever read; she couldn't wait to leave.

Nevertheless, she didn't jump at the first offer from another firm. Amusingly, it was the reverse of the situation she now had. The pay at the new firm would have been right and so would her supervisors and co-workers, but the work would not have been. As irritated as she was with people surrounding her, she decided not to take the offer. However, when no other jobs came her way in the next two weeks, she became jumpy. "That was a good position," she said anxiously, "and I let it go. I shouldn't have." Another week rolled by, and by then she had firmly made up her mind: "I'll never find another job like that one."

They hadn't hired anyone else yet, and were glad she was interested. Four months after she made the switch, she was miserable. "Before, my boss was boring. Here, the work is." She had known it, yet was so intent upon getting to the top as quickly as she could, she forgot it and scared herself into taking a job which could not have interested her less. Eight months after starting, she quit.

The important point here is that, rather than being an isolated event in Jennifer's life, it recurs regularly. If she sees something she wants, she immediately convinces herself that, "If I don't grab it, someone else will. Then they'll get there and I won't."

Bert is the same way. Most things don't interest him, but those which do make him feel edgy. He had gone shopping for a refrigerator, and having looked at a large number of models from different manufacturers, was uncertain about which, if any, was the best in his price range.

At a major discount appliance store, he found one the size he was seeking, and in an attractive color, as well. The price was $75 lower than comparable units he had seen. "It's on sale," he was told by the salesman. "That's a rock-bottom price." Bert liked what he saw, but considered looking further: "I wanted a name brand." The salesman then told him, "They're hard to get. We have only two left, and they'll probably both be gone by this afternoon." Bert bought it.

Two weeks after it was delivered he noticed a full-page ad in a newspaper featuring the same unit at a large nearby department store—for $100 less than the price he had paid. Remembering the salesman's words about how "hard to get" the units were, he called the department store, thinking they had just a few. "No," he was told by the manager of the appliance department, who had answered the phone, "we have over 120 of them. When we run a full-page ad, we *have* to have plenty of stock on hand. We don't want to be accused of bait-and-switch." Bert hung up the phone, furious. "I've been taken again," he fumed. "The whole world is full of bastards who just want to rip you off."

Perhaps. But whether their number be large or small, we are certainly each doing all we can to make their attempts to victimize us easier. In Chapter 7, we saw that most people think of their financial dealings as being divided into only two categories: consumption and investment. Few felt comfortable with the concept of investing in themselves. What makes matters far worse is that they frequently confuse the two categories they are comfortable with, and somehow roll consumption and investment into one.

Advertisers are helping them. Carpets, cars, furs, and silverware are now being sold as "investments." And people do indeed believe it, though they don't know why. "This rug has been a real investment," said Marjorie, beaming. "I've had it for fourteen years and it's still in excellent condition." What she means, of course, is that it was a good value for the money —a different matter entirely—and was a quality product, one which she felt good about owning.

It cost her $1,400, is now worth $400, and didn't have to be replaced three times during that period with carpeting which cost $500 each time and later became worthless. Interestingly, Marjorie's stocks have done about as well as her carpet, and have sunk to $9,000 from the $30,000 they cost her. She is definitely not pleased.

"They were an awful investment," she said. "How come?" we asked. "Because they are worth less now than when I bought them." Yet, as she firmly insists, "Everything I buy for my home has to be the best. I'm investing in the way I live."

It's no accident that so many of the people we studied confuse the two categories, consumption and investment. The thinking, never made conscious, runs as follows: "Every penny I spend on consumption is an investment. And my investments are going to make me rich."

"We've got to buy this car," said Al. "But it's more than we can afford," said Jane. "But look at the amount we're saving," he responded. "No one else is going to give us a discount this big." Al later admitted that he didn't really need the car at all, and without the offer of such "huge savings" would not have considered the purchase seriously.

The statements may seem somewhat contradictory, but there is method to Al's and Marjorie's madness. They are harboring a dream, one shared by more of the people we studied than any other: they would like to spend their way to wealth.

If that sounds absurdly contradictory, it is only because you see spending and saving, consuming and investing, as two, separate categories. And they don't.

They want desperately to become rich. Why? "So I can spend it, of course." And how are they going to become rich? "By investing," they say. Well then, what could be more fantastic and wonderful than spending your way to riches, something that would indeed happen if your spending *were* investing.

Few of the people we studied were crazy, and they tried to give some reality to their fantasy. Signs such as "Save 50 percent" allowed them to do just that. Do you know what the sign really means? It signifies that if you believed the sign and bought the item, only 50 percent of your money was spent, the other half was saved. And since it was saved it was invested, and having been invested, it's clearly going to grow and make you rich.

"But you didn't put any money in the bank, dear."

"No, but we left it there. We didn't have to take it out and spend it."

"But we don't have any money in the bank, we've been buying so many things at a discount."

"Doesn't matter. Think about what we've saved. An investment that large can't help but make us rich."

The more of a Stage Two-first orientation people had, the more likely they were to engage in such wishful and happily confused thinking. Their frequent comments about how much they've saved may make them seem like tightfisted bargain hunters, but they are merely impatient investors, wanting to spend. And save. And spend 'n' save. All in one.

LONGING FOR INVESTMENT CAPITAL

To most of the people we studied, a precise definition of "investment" is irrelevant. Whatever the word means, the distinction between it and consumption has been lost for them.

"I bought a chunk of jade," said Sid, getting up to get it. "Let me show it to you." He brought back a jade block. "It cost a bundle," he said proudly. Including fees and tax, its price was $1,510. He had also recently purchased a new couch, and the sofa and block were described in the same way. Basically, they were new toys, conversation pieces for the entertainment of his dinner guests.

That he wasn't earning any interest on the jade didn't bother him. Nor did he seem to care that it would have to rise substantially in price for him just to break even as of the day he'd bought it, thanks to the fee and tax he paid. "Is it an investment?" we asked. "It sure is," he said, "a serious one. At this price, it *has* to be."

Lynn felt similarly about the new World War I leather aviator's hat she bought in a nearby boutique. "It was $55, but it's worth it. I also bought a gas mask. There aren't many of these old hats left nowadays." The owner of the shop she had purchased it from later laughed when he heard it. "We put out only a few at a time," he said, "but we've got lots of them in back. They come in large cartons."

People with both a Stage Two-first orientation *and* a confused view of consumption and investment were the ones who really went wild. And in order to see how, when, and why they did, it's worth our while to study how an investment craze generally works.

Suppose in 1910 the glass-manufacturing firm of Thomas Tentoes (pronounced, "ten toes") started producing dinner plates in upstate New York at an average rate of a million a year. Just before World War II, he quit, having manufactured a total of 30 million of them, all exactly the same; old man Tentoes never varied a thing. There were so many of the plates floating around, they caught no one's hungry eye. They were just used. And dropped, and chipped and cracked, until there were only 3 million of them left.

Although they too were available "by the carton," and most junk dealers priced them cheaply at 25 to 75 cents apiece, a few tried getting $1.50 for them, and on occasion, got it. Children who'd grown up in homes where the plates were used, however, didn't have to wait until one broke before throwing it away. "I was tired of looking at them," said Dennis, "and when we moved, we threw them out." Soon the number of plates was well below a million, and dealers everywhere were getting $1 to $2 apiece for them.

We don't know who was the first to realize the plates were fast disappearing. Perhaps a few dealers and individuals realized it simultaneously. Whatever the case, a few months later prices for the plates began at $3, and they were indeed becoming harder to find. At that point, a large dealer boosted the price to $10 each, and it stuck. "I figured I'd jack it up," he said, "and see if we sell any." He did. The higher price spread quickly, and so did word that the plates had become rare.

It was then, and only then, that thousands of people who previously hadn't had 2 cents' worth of interest in the plates suddenly developed an intense desire to pay $15 to $25 apiece for them. Why? "They're pretty," one said. "They're old," said another. Both then added, "And besides, they're a good investment."

Prior to that time, we'd been unable to find even one person who thought the plates were attractive. In fact, most people had long considered old man Tentoes' plates downright ugly. But the new buyers were seeing the price as well as the plate, and as one put it, "How good-looking is a $100 bill?", the value he soon expected the plate to attain.

Most of the buyers we talked to found that attitude a bit crass. While readily acknowledging they considered the plates an investment, they also claimed to like them "for themselves." And they meant it. Yet the fact remains that the overwhelming majority of people who had bought the plates had not done so until a public impression of scarcity had been created.

A newspaper column, reporting upon the reawakened interest in the old plates, attributed it to "nostalgia." "These young people long for a world they've left behind, long for old-fashioned values." Maybe. But greed is also an old-fashioned value. And its presence became clear when some of the owners of the plates heard that another 3 million of them had been found in an old warehouse in Albany and they were now once again worth 25 cents each instead of the $25 many had paid. No small number suddenly then said, "I'm not surprised. I always thought those things were an eyesore."

We've been discussing dinner plates, but a similar situation prevailed where hundreds of different "investments" were concerned: old eyeglasses, radios, records and record players, jukeboxes, clothes, furniture, comic books, watches, jewelry, dolls, bottles, toys, pens and ink stands, flags, posters, buttons, rusty anchors and nautical gear, pipes, blankets and tablecloths, kitchen utensils, farm tools, washtubs, catalogues, apothecary jars, magazines, serving trays, hats, autographs, canes, cuff links, garters, uniforms, furs, cameras, microscopes, telescopes and binoculars, barber poles, chairs and shaving supplies, pillboxes and compacts, seltzer bottles, Tiffany and kerosene lamps, barometers, weather vanes, swords, knives, guns, and armor.

With each, at some point an impression of scarcity became widespread and electrified the public. In a frenzy, many attempted to obtain at least one of the currently hottest items on the list. Prices soared as the number of people pouring into the market for the product increased dramatically.

Lo and behold, there were always more than enough of each item to go around, assuming you were willing to pay the prevailingly high price.

Soon, though, the market was saturated: everyone who wanted one had one. They may have paid through the nose to get it, but they had gotten it. And then what happened? They left, to go looking for their fortune elsewhere.

The decreasing number of people who were interested in actively bidding for the item did not, however, cause its price to decrease. It stayed high, but the market for the item thinned considerably. Only "serious collectors" remained. The price boom was over. Amusingly, it was an investment only briefly—namely, during the period when it was rapidly rising in price. After that, it became a dust collector in tens of thousands of homes and apartments. The next wave would be along as soon as an impression of scarcity could attach itself to another common product. That, together with some confusion about consumption vs. investment and a Stage Two-first orientation, is all it takes to set off a stampede. Those are the three ingredients of an investment craze.

Is anything wrong with what the enormous number of people who spend (save?) in this way are doing? Shouldn't they buy all the nice old things they become interested in?

If their intention is to become wealthy, the answer is definitely "no." First of all, by the time they even notice the item, everyone else has already noticed it, too. As it becomes the subject of a flurry of articles, radio and TV comments, and much living room conversation, they are hearing about it at the worst possible time: they buy "at the top" and wind up paying far too high a price. Remember, it's no investment if the price, at best, stays where it is, and at worst, starts falling, as the many excited buyers who crowded into the market leave.

Secondly, not only do they buy at the top, they also hang on. They were confused from the start about whether they were spending or saving, consuming or investing, so they don't rush to sell if its value then begins to decrease. For that reason, its price doesn't usually plummet. By contrast, a stock which faddishly soars will subsequently sink, because it was bought strictly as an investment and sooner or later (usually later) will be dumped if it doesn't do well. Tentoes' plates didn't drop in price once the bulk of buyers had finished grabbing them up, because the mob of buyers didn't then turn around and turn into a mob of sellers.

And finally, not only had they paid top dollar for a product whose price stayed flat or gently fell, and which yielded no annual rate of return, they also succeeded in tying up a lot of the money they might otherwise have used for serious investing. The percentages here were nothing short of astonishing.

People who chronically complained they didn't have enough money with which to make a major investment nonetheless often spent half or more of the surplus income they received each month on Tentoes' plates and a wide variety of spend 'n' save items. They were unable to start saving money —with the intention of later investing it—because by their unconscious reasoning, they already were. The investment capital they longed for was right under their nose (or should we say, "between their knife and fork") in a Tentoes' plate they secretly hoped would one day make them rich.

In short, the severely shrunken estimate they had of their available investment capital, and the top prices they paid for non-interest-bearing assets which they did not subsequently dispose of, made them feel much poorer than they actually were. Their main goal was to become rich—and the sooner, the better—but in spraying their investment monies in a dozen different directions, they prevented themselves from using investing as a way of getting there.

Just as they'd hoped, though, no one called them greedy. After all, they were merely buying things which, as one put it, "are both fun and have value." Whatever pleasure they derived from their "fun investments," they became more desperate then ever as a result of them. "I just want to be rich," one said in exasperation. "Is that so much to ask?" Whenever an opportunity presented itself, it thus *had* to be pounced upon. There was no time to lose: there might never be another one like it.

LOCAL COLOR

In spite of their confused attitude toward spending and saving —and the kinds of purchases they were thus led to make— most of the people we studied finally accumulated what they considered to be investment capital. "In this bank account, I keep my rainy day money," said Tina, "and in this one, money for investing." And since that is how they viewed it, that is how they used it. Impulsively. Crazed hunters shoot at anything which moves; crazed investors do the same, only instead they throw money. And as we shall see, they feel they have an exceptionally good reason for doing so.

Tina is employed by a large broadcasting company, and although she still finds the work glamorous after fourteen years with the firm, her pay isn't. "The fringe benefits are good," she says, "but I never get to put anything away." Her mother died when Tina was twelve, and four years ago her father also died, leaving her and her brother a net of $106,000 each. It was the first lump sum Tina had ever had. She decided to keep $56,000 as rainy day money and use the other $50,000 as investment capital.

That she even made a conscious decision to divide the money in this way was unusual. Unfortunately, most people simply don't think about it. If they are feeling cocky or rushed, all their available funds are classified as investment capital. And when they are scared, it all becomes money for a rainy day (which they then think will be arriving tomorrow). Most of the time, though, they are somewhere in between: some portion is set aside as a safety cushion and the remainder is to be used for investing—and how the breakdown varies from month to month is a good indication of how buoyant or fearful they feel at the time.

The thought Tina had given to the matter was atypical. The way she then proceeded to invest her money was not.

It is important to remind yourself that some of the seemingly most reasonable people you'll ever meet—intelligent, soft-spoken, well mannered, and hardworking—are absolutely nuts when it comes to their investment activities. Behind the façade of rationality there usually sits someone intensely dedicated to Stage Two first. That emerges most clearly when you see who is actually playing the lunatic fringe issues which happen to be popular at any given moment in the stock market. If you are expecting someone who looks like an escaped mental patient, forget it. Only the things these fine-looking folks do with their money allows us to see the thick layer of loony lava bubbling just beneath the surface.

What they do in investment areas other than stocks is equally rabid, but not nearly as visible. The houses they buy which turn out to be poor investments don't usually disappear; shoddy stocks often do, with millions watching. Tina, in particular, decided to buy some real estate with her investment capital. She skis, and it was natural for her to consider using the money to buy a vacation home.

"I'm there Christmas, Washington's Birthday, and most weekends," she said, "and when I'm not, I could rent it out." So far so good; similar thoughts have helped convince an enormous number of people to buy second homes, in shore and mountain areas. But it didn't stop there: which property she wound up buying, and why, is of great importance, because so many others did what she did, and for the same reason.

There has been a startling change over the last twenty years in the real estate purchases of the people we studied. Twenty years ago, those buying houses in the mountains, say, were forced to choose one of the small number of offerings available. Few were for sale, since most of the people who lived then in what are now resort towns had been there a long time and had no intention of moving. "When I die, I'll leave," said one, age eighty-six, speaking for the rest.

But the rapidly growing number of city dwellers who wanted "a place of my own in the country" weren't about to wait for someone to die before they could find one. Local builders, sensing the growing demand, attempted to meet it. Slowly, since their financial resources were modest, "and besides," one added, "I have to live with these people." The "locals," as they were called by the new arrivals, weren't thrilled about the flurry of houses springing up—however slowly—all around them.

At some point, more experienced developers moved in. In a significant number of cases, the new developers were burning their candles at both ends. They had moved to the area full time to retire, or vacationed there regularly, because they found it attractive, and as one put it, "so different from the congestion in the city." And yet, they could see the need for new housing, and the opportunity that that created, far better than the locals could. "It's as easy as falling off a log," said one, of his weekend development activities. "Next to what I do in the city, this is small potatoes." They themselves were in large part going to be responsible for erasing the small-town atmosphere which had drawn them there in the first place.

They were going to have plenty of help, on both ends of the spectrum. Many individuals simply bought land and tried building their own vacation dream houses. They didn't need or want anyone to help them. Even though they made any number of minor and occasionally major blunders in getting the house built, "at least it is mine," one said proudly. "I did it myself."

For those with less pioneer spirit or time, major corporations, as well as individuals, were also building. As the people newly arriving in town swelled from a trickle to a roaring river, the larger developers took over. "We *have* to have the demand, the traffic, the customers," said the President of a sizable construction firm, "even if that means we're Johnny-come-latelies on the scene."

At times, it seemed that everyone was in the construction or real estate business. The local yellow pages listed enough brokers and builders to make you think you were in the largest suburb of a major city. Perhaps that is inevitable, though, when a town has more houses than inhabitants and more tourists than residents.

Tina thus wound up buying a house that had never been owned by locals. It hadn't been erected with them in mind, either. Instead, it was erected by tourists, for tourists. That may not strike you as a particularly revolting fact, but judged by the lengths to which everyone involved with the sale of such a property goes to hide it, it must be.

Tina looked at some older houses, too. But as she put it, "They had charm, and space, and a *lot* of problems." They hadn't been built for a wealthy clientele to begin with, and the quality of materials and assembly left much to be desired. The area had not been rich until the tourists came. And the houses were erected less as palaces than as basic shelter; little that was fancy or costly was used, since the locals at the time were hard-pressed to pay for them, as it was.

And over the years, the houses had taken a beating. Sea- or lakeside housing, whipped by wind blowing hard across the water, had been exposed to many of the same stresses those in mountain areas had. The snow and cold made the problems even worse. The weather had taken its toll on the paint, porches, and roofs. Tina had the plumbing, heating, and electrical systems checked by an engineer, and found them at best in need of repair, and more often, in need of replacement and modernization.

That made a new house a very reasonable choice. Like older houses, the quality of its materials and assembly also left much to be desired, "but at least it's new," said Tina, "and new is new," a difficult point to debate. Yet it was apparent right from the start that practical considerations would play only a minor role in the marketing of new housing. After all, the customers weren't just buying a house. They were buying the area as well, which is what made them want a house there in the first place.

"Local color" was thus loudly hawked along with the house. It hadn't occurred to those locals who were interested in selling their homes to use themselves as their own best advertisement. They were too busy living their lives to step outside them and use a folksy depiction as a sales tool. It would have felt to them like an act of self-parody.

As it turned out, they didn't have to do it to themselves; others saw them as caricatures, anyway. A couple from the city answered an ad placed directly by an elderly couple eager to sell their house and move to a warmer part of the country. "Arizona, or Florida, maybe," the woman said. "We can't take the cold anymore." The youngsters went through the motions of looking at the house, but found themselves more interested in the old couple. After leaving, the young man said, "Now *that's* a pair of locals for you." And she replied, "You're not kidding." Then they both laughed uncomfortably.

The yawning gap separating the two couples was more than a generational one. It was cultural, as well. They had little common ground, and no way to bridge the vast distance dividing them except to talk about the business at hand. According to the youngsters, it was the way the locals lived that was so attractive. "We want to be part of it," they said. Most newcomers met few, if any, old-timers. But those who did knew without ever saying so that that could never be the case.

Once the new arrivals settled in, they often looked more like locals than the locals themselves did. Cowboy hats, boots, and trucks, or in other locations, bib overalls and wool plaid work shirts. Fishermen, farmers, ranchers, and store owners all proved blessedly easy to imitate. Donning the right clothes, walk, and accent, it wasn't hard to make yourself feel you were successfully portraying the genuine (pronounced "jen-you-wine") article. "Who, me?" said one particularly effective young masquerader. "I've been here 100 years." When all is said and done, the new arrivals didn't want "the real thing." They wanted a healthier and cleaned-up version of it, one which would make them comfortable because the people in it were familiar. It wasn't the locals they were interested in impressing—they secretly knew that that was out of the question—it was people like themselves. Each tried to "outlocal" the others.

Developers knew what the new customers wanted, and gave it to them—but good. Neil spent twelve years in a major eastern city, first as a securities and then a commodities broker. Although his income varied considerably from year to year, on average he made a decent living and managed to put $80,000 away. Together with a friend of his, who had been in advertising and who had saved a somewhat smaller amount, Neil moved to a western ski town and became a developer. "We decided to build condominiums," he said, "and sell them to the weekenders." Most of the buildings in the area were

Pueblo style, and Neil felt it was a wise choice to continue that tradition. "We knew it would make it easier to sell the units," he said.

Tina's first few conversations with Neil were similar to those hundreds of others that the people we studied initially had had with the developers, brokers, and owners who sold them the units they bought. The pitch was exceedingly simple: "This place is a paradise, and you're lucky to be here before it's discovered by the masses."

Tina's own experience in the parking lot at the base of the ski hill, where people were often ready to kill for any remaining parking spots, should have told her something. Forget for the moment the number of cars looking for spots, the number of skiers searching at mealtimes for seats in local restaurants, and the long lines at the ski lifts. The very fact that there was someone from the city who was now building condominiums for people also from the city should have telegraphed loudly and clearly that, far from being undiscovered, the place was fast becoming congested and overpriced.

It was easy, however, for her to ignore the evidence staring her right in the face. Like thousands of others who were flocking to the area, she saw what she wanted to see. For her $56,000, she got a one-bedroom, one-and-a-half-bath condominium which looked as though it would not survive a solid sneeze.

Neil isn't evil, and Tina is no fool. They, and similar pairs all across the country, simply conspired together unwittingly to create a fiction. It may have been fun, but it was no investment—not for Tina, at any rate, or for the 191 of 1,057 who made similar purchases elsewhere. And not for Neil, either: an old couple who had sold him the land he was developing were the ones who really made out like bandits. They had paid $40 an acre for it in June 1941. Thirty years later they sold him the 104 acres for $2,500 per acre.

Insofar as the people who bought vacation homes were happy to have them, experienced a certain pride of ownership, and liked the convenience of knowing where they'd be staying each time, fine. Yet, in more than 82 percent of the instances, the owners viewed their purchase primarily as an investment. In that case, it was a poor one. For when all the costs of ownership are weighed against the various financial benefits, the large majority would have found it cheaper to invest their money at 9 percent per annum elsewhere and stay in a lodge.

There were individual cases in which a vacation home, bought as an investment, did well as an investment. On balance, however, it was people who bought properties they liked very much, in areas which brokers and developers weren't yet loudly labeling as a "good investment," who did best. Tourists who knew they had come there for the seashore, lake, mountains, or skiing, and not for a real estate windfall, were more, not less, likely to find it. Unconsciously, they realized that the fewer "authentic" people there are left in an area, the more heavily "local color" will be used to promote the place.

SHOPPING FOR AUTHENTICITY

The investment purchases of the people we studied displayed a very disturbing pattern. Its outline slowly became clear only as the number of transactions being examined grew quite large.

Earlier we saw that it was common for people to confuse spending and saving, consumption and investment, since that allowed them to give reality to a widely held financial fantasy: that somehow it's possible to spend your way to wealth instead of welfare. The result was that a considerable portion of each person's capital was spent on "fun investments"— collectibles which had briefly radiated an impression of scarcity, had been snapped up by newly eager buyers, and were now collecting dust instead of interest in millions of apartments and homes.

Almost without exception, the people making such purchases felt they were buying "a piece of history." And they were, although greed played a significant motivating role. What was striking, however, is that people buying vacation homes in such places as Stowe, Jackson, Taos, Sun Valley, Aspen, the Hamptons, Nantucket, the Cape, and shore and lake areas everywhere, were saying the same thing. There was remarkably little difference between the comments they made about a bent and dented old brass looking glass and a house or condo in beach or ski country.

How could that be? It seemed impossible that someone buying a newly built condominium would see it as being scarce. And that, being in some way "a piece of history," it had to be "grabbed quickly, before there are none left." Once again, the most prevalent explanation offered, often by the buyers themselves, was that, as one put it, "You never can tell if any more of these will be available." Not even the knowledge that the developer had plans to build more units, once those currently being offered were sold, calmed the frenzy surrounding the decision.

It has frequently been noted that everyone wants to be the last person to move into a quaint little town. "Now that *I'm* here," said one quite openly, "I hope they stop letting people in." Rather than being the whole story, it is now clear that that attitude is merely the tip of a hugh iceberg: a search for authenticity.

The purchasers of telescopes, or country houses to hold them, were looking above all to buy what they think others have and they themselves don't. Neil knows he isn't one of the natives, woodchucks, old-timers, Indians, farmers, ranchers, cowboys, or red-necks. But he'd like to be, for two reasons: in his mind it would make him authentic. Besides making him feel good, he'd then have some genuine authenticity to sell, e.g., to Tina, who is as interested in it as he. Thus together they play "let's pretend." He sells and she buys what they both know can't really be bought or sold.

Nevertheless, both are aware that if something is rare and a growing number of people want it, it will fetch a high price.

So they try hard to obtain some of what, to them, is exceedingly scarce and is indeed in great demand: authenticity.

But why in the world do they need it? Because they, like the overwhelming majority, are Stage Two first. They want to be rich. Then they'll do what their inner urgings prompt them to do. Decades are rolling by while they remain severely detached from themselves, awaiting the arrival of great wealth before they can become what they know they are, but without money cannot yet be.

Few things pull you outside yourself so forcibly and completely as a Stage Two-first orientation. Fewer still will cause you to spend a lifetime there. In addition to the major effect it has on other facets of people's lives, it makes their investment actions impulsive and unprofitable. And that is particularly distressing, since they never stop hoping that a spectacularly profitable investment will one day allow them to at last be themselves.

PART THREE

CHAPTER TWELVE

Where Are You Now?—
Self-assessment Questions
Everyone Should Ask

Seeing what others do, and finding out why they did it, is interesting. But it's time to determine what relevance the success or failure of the people we studied has for you.

The most effective way to compare their hopes and experiences with your own is through a series of questions.

QUESTION ONE. How much do you like your work?

This seemingly simple question is the one people most often lied about when answering. The best way to see why is to consider what would happen to you if you were in jail. Not for a crime you committed, of course; it was a case of mistaken identity. But there you are, anyway.

All around you are people who want to get out, people who would give anything to escape. Some would definitely kill—you—if that would help. However, unbeknown to them, your situation is unlike theirs in two crucial respects. First, you are secretly being paid handsomely to be there. And second, as opposed to all the others, you like it. You enjoy the place and the life it allows you to live.

Now comes the key question: Do you dare tell that to the others?

Everyone depicts the world around them differently. By far, the characterization offered most frequently by those who didn't like their work was that the world is a jail. In essence, they felt they were living in a prison without walls. Without realizing it, they described first one workplace, then another, and then a third, all as cells without bars.

Their repeated use of the image tells us they really hated their work, not the place. If they were having sex there, or were similarly absorbed, they'd not have noticed what, in any event, was usually a nice-looking work setting. However, from their deep discontent sprang a fair amount of cruelty.

When they saw someone who they sensed was content, they labeled the person "a zombie," "a cow," or "dull," and often unconsciously attempted to be disruptive. One who openly loathed her job said of another happily working two desks away, "Look at little goody-two-shoes over there, hoping for a promotion," and of a third, "Who, her? She's a real climber."

Those who enjoyed their work thus quickly learned to keep their mouths shut. As one put it, "I told two of the people I work with that I'm happy here, and now they think I'm crazy. They just refused to believe it." Both to avoid ridicule and rejection, and on the positive side, to gain a certain measure of acceptance and belonging, people who were involved with their work soon became good at lying.

The trouble with telling a lie too often, however, is that in time you yourself come to believe it. It was amazing to see people who thoroughly enjoyed their work suddenly saying the reverse to people who hated theirs.

"Your work is boring?" one said. "Well, mine is too." Call it politeness, or being agreeable, but it had a detrimental effect. Instead of merely being deliberately deceitful because they liked their work and didn't want others to know it, they went a giant step further and started bitching every bit as loudly and often as the people around them. They began by fooling others; they wound up fooling themselves. It's understandable, though; they didn't want to be outcasts, much less attacked by the other prisoners—I mean, workers.

Besides, they did indeed have something to complain about. Since they profoundly enjoyed their work, the two hours, say, they spent caught up in it seemed to them more like forty minutes. Rather than marveling at that fact, they instead came to the opposite conclusion. "I'm not doing enough work," said one. "I've only been at it for a few minutes." We encountered the phenomenon repeatedly: the more people loved and got lost in their work—and hence lost track of time—the less of it they thought they had done. So they became annoyed, primarily with themselves.

On the other hand, those who weren't particularly fond of their work also had something to complain about. To them, two hours of it seemed like four, or even eight. They too became annoyed, with whoever it was that, in their view, was forcing them to work.

The two may have been complaining about different things, but it was fun to watch them smoothly carry on a conversation, each oblivious to the difference. "He's a real bastard," said one about their boss. "Yeah, I know what you mean," said the other. "Nothing is ever good enough. I do my best and it's *still* not good enough." The latter person appears to be talking about what the boss finds acceptable, but in fact, it is she herself who isn't satisfied with the quantity and quality of the work she loves doing, work which the former one resents doing at all. The complaints of the two arise from exactly opposite sources, but their conversation isn't hampered by it in the least.

The air is full of an enormous number of such conversations each day, and growing youngsters have no way of telling which of the complaints they hear are camouflage and which represent real resentment. You, as an adolescent and young adult, could hardly have escaped being exposed to a shower of complaints by people about their work. It is difficult for anyone exposed to many years of such bombardment to distinguish who really hates their work (and is only too happy to let you know it), and who loves theirs (and is afraid to say so). Both say the same things about it.

Nevertheless, it is of major importance for you to be able to tell when people are lying to you about their work. Because the evidence points overwhelmingly to the fact that work you enjoy is far more likely to make you rich than will any investment you make.

We need a name for what's going on here, and a good one is: "the Millionaire's Lie." People who are wealthy have valid reason for not telling you how much they are worth. After all, when you've got plenty, you've got plenty to lose. Yet, those who eventually became millionaires would have been more willing to tell you their bank balance than to acknowledge how much their work meant to them.

Why were they so prone to mask their involvement? To paraphrase: When you've got plenty, you've got plenty to hide. The Millionaire's Lie consists of a deep and continuing work-interest which is publicly denied ("Who, me? Nah. I hate my work, too, just as much as you do.") because that enjoyment was the real source of their wealth. It was therefore mandatory for them to prevent the other prisoners from attacking it and taking it away. Lost money could always be re-earned and replaced, but someone who stripped them of their involvement with their work would have wound up killing the goose which laid the golden eggs.

Learning how to tell when people are lying to you about how much their work means to them will allow you to take the next step: learning how to tell when you are lying to others, and to yourself, about how deeply involved you are with your own activities. Some of the prisoners out there are undeniably vicious, and no one should feel ashamed of the fact that they have learned how to lie in order to protect something they love from being attacked.

Unfortunately, the vast majority of people overdo it. They

want so much to decrease their vulnerability to attack, they bury their intense involvement under countless layers of phony indifference and counterfeit annoyance. They are well defended, all right. But defending themselves has consumed them, leaving little left for offense, for wholeheartedly doing the things they enjoy.

Not only does a posture that defensive cost them the enjoyment they'd otherwise have had, it also pushes them to make a drastic mistake. They have come to believe their own and everyone else's complaints about work, and hence they long for and lunge for money. The principal harm done them by their belief in their own and everyone else's lies is that they feel forced to first become wealthy. Then, as one put it, "I'll do only the jobs *I* feel like doing."

The trouble with trying to leap over the work and land on the reward is that it backfires badly. In case after case, those who attempted to overlook the work and seize the wealth merely gambled away their incoming paychecks and frivolously used any money they had already accumulated on harebrained and speculative "investments" they hoped would be instantly and spectacularly profitable. Ironically, all they succeeded in doing was to cut themselves off from the only vehicle which stood a decent chance of making them rich in the first place.

QUESTION TWO. Specifically, how can I tell if I like my work?

There are three ways. The first is to see how you'd feel if you were prevented from doing it. Any number of people who told us they hated their work suddenly realized they had other, more positive feelings as well, once they were told that, in their own best interests, they'd henceforth be prohibited from engaging in the activity they found so objectionable.

It is worth your while to spend a few minutes considering what your life would be like if you couldn't do the kind of work you now do. (Remember, we're talking about your

work, not your job; a similar type of work at a different firm
—perhaps your own—or in a different setting, with different
people, might prove substantially more satisfying.) In time,
you'd probably adjust to any such prohibition and find something else you enjoyed doing. But how would you feel in the
interim? Frequent responses were, "I'd feel like a fish out of
water"; "This is the only thing I really know how to do,"
and, "Right now, I couldn't earn much of a living doing anything else."

The last reply is one we shouldn't take too lightly. Locating
another line of work which would pay you the same as your
present one does would in most instances not be easy. An accountant, say, who grows tired of his occupation and wants to
become a physicist or brain surgeon obviously can't just snap
his fingers and have it happen. Retraining would be a long and
expensive process. "And anyway," many added, "I don't want
to be a thirty-five-year-old student."

As it turned out, there was no reason to be. Rarely was it a
mere coincidence that people were doing the kind of work
which currently employed them. They often said, "I just
stumbled into this job," or, "It was only by chance that I
began doing this." Most meant it when they said it. Yet, there
are nowhere near as many such "accidents" as they would
have you believe.

First of all, viewed from inside themselves, their lives do
seem full of isolated events which "appear from out of nowhere." But when viewed with some perspective, there are
regularities, consistencies, and important patterns which are
easily seen. And second, attributing your present line of work
to "luck" stops anyone from digging deeper to find out how
much your work means to you.

Since the line of work people were doing was no accident
—and in fact, they had to ignore a number of other opportunities which came their way in order to do it—a minor shift
in their focus often produced a significant increase in the degree to which they were caught up by it. Notice we said
"caught up," not "liked" or "loved." Beware of anyone who

tells you they love their work. There are an enormous number of people who are devoting their lives to one-upping others: whatever you have, they have to convince you they have something better. Telling them you like your work will make them say they love theirs. If they can lord it over others, they do. The fact that on many an occasion it dangerously antagonized some of the more murderous prisoners was something these insecure bigmouths ignored at their own later expense. Few of the people who were absorbed by their work *ever* said so. And the more captivated they were, the more of a smoke screen of silence and casualness they usually adopted for public display.

A second way to gauge how much you like your work is to think about how much of it you'd do if you knew you'd be dead in five years. If your life were coming to an end, is it the way you'd want to be spending the time you've got left?

Many of the people who eventually became millionaires not only said "yes," they added, "I'd do even more of it than I'm doing now." Rather than changing fields, they said they would rid their current activities of a lot of administrative, secretarial, organizational, and distracting matters which were, as one put it, "responsible for keeping me from being my best as often as I'd like."

If you, on the other hand, feel your current job is, as one put it, "the equivalent of already being dead," you do indeed need to do something about it. People in your position spent far more time dreaming about finding an instant fortune than others did. However, the results show they were significantly less likely to actually find it.

The third, and by far the most powerful tool for deciding whether or not you like your work is to think about how much the pettier aspects of it annoy you. Nothing in reality is only grand; trivial details abound and are a major part of everything you do. However, the more you enjoy your work, the less likely you are to notice them.

Two problems need mentioning. The first is that you have to actively be doing something before you can assess how irritated its more trivial aspects will make you. If you are in sales and would rather be a biochemist or pilot, you can't simply sit down and decide how annoying its pedestrian dimensions are. You have to be doing the activity.

Moreover, you have to have done it for a while. In the beginning, the details connected with any activity loom large. A man who is now an outstanding tennis player borrowed someone else's racket for the second game he ever played. It had too small a grip, something he didn't notice until he went to slam back a high lob. The racket went farther than the ball. He found himself quite annoyed that a detail such as grip size had to be attended to at all. Similarly, beginning skiers initially find the strange equipment they have on their hands and feet their greatest hazard. Later, as experts, they told us they almost forget it was there, and concentrated instead on the terrain's variation and the snow conditions.

The second problem with the irritation index is this: instead of being annoyed at your work, you might be just annoyed—and are taking it out on your work. From time to time, that happens to everyone; something angers them and the pettier aspects of their work suddenly seem a major nuisance.

One day's reading thus won't do. How you react on average, day in and day out, week in and week out, is the relevant reading. The fact that the average daily level of irritation you experience is high *still* doesn't mean it is your work which is generating it. There are a large number of people who are mad at almost everything, almost every day. For them, obtaining an accurate reading of how much in particular their work annoyed them was nearly impossible. If that applies to you, get help. Walking around angry is costing you more than you realize. You also need to consider the possibility that your boss and/or co-workers are upsetting you. See if limiting contact with certain ones, or avoiding them altogether, if you can, improves matters. In many instances, it produced a significant change.

It turns out that most people can tell which of the two is responsible for annoying them: the work itself or the people they work with. Regardless of which it is, do something about it. Particularly if it is the work itself, our results show clearly that in putting up with the situation, in the long run you're not doing yourself any financial favor.

QUESTION THREE. But what if the work I enjoy doesn't pay very well?

A substantial number of people made comments such as, "I like my work, but what bothers me is that it'll never make me rich." That is bunk. You would be shocked to discover how wide a variety of businesses and activities have made people wealthy. Everything from wood dowels to popcorn.

There is an important reason why so large a portion of the public has come to the false conclusion that their own work won't make them rich: they harbor the wildly mistaken notion that only gold mines, oil and gas, real estate, and stocks produce great wealth. Although at one time that may in part have been the case, it is definitely not so any longer. Essentially, the public is confusing the rain and the reservoir—the latter is merely a catch basin for the former. In short, the bulk of someone's fortune may now wind up flowing into buildings, bonds, and stocks. But that is rarely what produced the fortune in the first place.

The misconception is a monumentally costly one. It results in millions of people belittling their work and privately perceiving their own efforts as puny.

Those who eventually became millionaires were especially good at masking the profound involvement they had with their work. They themselves knew it, but they almost never told anyone else about it. Interestingly, first they hid the degree to which they were enthralled, and then later, as a consequence, they had a substantial sum of money to hide. At that point, however, some chose to stop camouflaging both their involvement and their wealth. In most cases, it was a decision which was forced upon them by the pressure of the facts. Their expanding public position made it more difficult for them to mask how much their work meant to them.

Still, even though they were now letting down their guard, and had some assistance in protecting themselves against the other prisoners, they did not discuss the underlying dynamics. What they said instead was one word long. When they were asked what had made them so successful, they replied, "Persistence." As public figures now, trying to be honest and helpful, the word of advice they offered those who wanted to emulate them was "persist."

The fact remains, however, that no one can tell you to persist. If the work you are doing doesn't interest you enough to make you want to do it year in and year out—in spite of yourself—you won't do it. We are all incredibly skilled at finding a host of excuses for not doing something we don't feel like doing. Often, we simply forget, or allow something more intriguing to catch our eye.

Even the knowledge that doing something you detest will make you rich won't get you to do it. For a short period of time, it might. Yet the evidence shows that no matter how lustily someone talks (as many did) about "doing anything, and I mean anything, to become fabulously rich," they will become bored and fatigued by the whole business long before they are even halfway there.

Only one thing has shown itself clearly capable of taking you all the way there: your own involvement with a particular area or activity. If you want to label that, and hence yourself, as puny, go ahead. You'll find plenty of people only too happy to agree. Having you out of the running aids their own efforts; there is almost too much competition as it is. Nevertheless, only being quietly captivated will make you persist. Apparently, nothing else even comes close. Those who privately sneered at or mocked their own efforts pressured themselves into becoming modern Don Quixotes, attacking casinos instead of windmills; prepared to gamble on gold, ponies, and options—anything that glittered—but wound up feeling equally foolish and frustrated.

But what of the market for you and your efforts? Will there be any? Does being seized by your spine and held tight by an activity, year after year, guarantee that sooner or later someone besides you will pay attention to what you are doing? Perhaps not. Yet, almost without exception, those who eventually became millionaires were surprised, even stunned by what happened. "I've been doing this for *years*," one said, "and suddenly the world has gotten mighty interested." Remember, everything that made people wealthy in the past is just that: in the past. As experienced marketing people have learned, often at great expense, what the world loved yesterday it may have lost interest in completely by tomorrow. No matter how long you accidentally persist in doing something, the world may never beat a path to your door. But the only way you will ever give it a good chance to do so is to keep doing what you enjoy.

QUESTION FOUR. When and if the world comes knocking at my door, what will it be buying?

The rarest commodity of all, the one currently in shortest supply: authenticity. The majority of workers—593 of 1,057 (approximately 56 percent)—have lost hope that their work will bring them anything: satisfaction or wealth. So they take whichever job pays best, and for the most part, go through the motions. They are indeed good at it. As one put it, "I do what I have to, but that's all." Theirs is a polished performance, even if it completely lacks substance. Most know it, but try not to let it show. Some, however, now no longer care if it does. They resent having to do anything for you, no matter how small, and they want you to know it.

What is fascinating, though, is that those who openly hated their work, those who secretly loved theirs, and everyone in between were looking for the same thing: something real. Unless they were buying a product strictly for reasons of economy (for example, the cheapest gasoline or can of peas), they wanted more.

The deep, personal involvement someone had with their work was sought. They knew it wouldn't be obvious, or easy to find. Yet, the care shown its every facet, the depths of concern and long hours or even years it had taken to produce, the originality no superficial interest could ever have achieved, was something the customers desperately needed—those who hated their work even more than those who loved theirs.

Usually, what they got instead was the image of quality and a false impression of scarcity: the artist's signature—reproduced by a machine; the designer's name or initials—plastered all over a product manufactured in the Orient by a licensee; remakes of movies and records which had caught on; the warm and smiling face on a package, which off the package tells you bluntly, "The product is trash"; the illusion of craftsmanship in everything from pianos and stoves to cars and houses. Sales people marveled that, as one put it, "the suckers keep coming back for more." But the need was genuine, even if the products being served up to satisfy it were not.

Not having it, the customers had to buy it. Dizzyingly being caught up and captivated was something they could not live their lives without. A child's desire to be hypnotically engrossed doesn't end with childhood. Being absorbed is deeper and more important than like and dislike, love and hate. It is the only magic our everyday lives have left.

The public, having beaten a path to your door, won't ask for some of your involvement with your work. Not directly, anyway. Instead, they'll want some of the products or services they have heard you are outstanding at making or rendering. The fact that you've spent many years consumed by your work will have made what you do uncommon. (It won't seem that way to you. Without exception, every one of our millionaires was the last to realize how extraordinary they had become at their craft. Indeed, many knew they could do even better, and subsequently did.)

If you are worried about whether or not you'll have enough of yourself to go around at the time, don't be. Meeting the demand is easier than you imagine. Since most of the public can't afford the price of the original, and have grown accustomed to making do with a copy, at least for a while they will happily let you get away with franchising your authenticity. Then they will have no choice but to continue their search elsewhere.

QUESTION FIVE. If doing what I enjoy earns me less, won't the total amount I lose over the years be substantial?

Not necessarily. Instead of rising rapidly in the beginning and flattening out later, the earnings curves of most of those who eventually became millionaires was the reverse: their income increased slowly, if at all, for many years. And then, after two to three decades, it suddenly went through the roof. What they had lost prior to that time they more than recovered later.

As warehousing and shipping manager, the $15,000 salary Eric was paid was a number he found it hard to leave. The move to $24,000 took him eight years. Getting to $32,000 was even harder, and took him close to eleven years. That he was one of the best in the country at what he did was known to everyone in the business but Eric. Anything he could learn about inventory control, finding suitable personnel, materials handling, maintenance, trucking routes and schedules, billing and bookkeeping, he did. Things his bosses would never have even thought to ask him were done quietly and well, and the areas of business for which he was responsible were conspicuous by the minimum of problems which developed there.

Nevertheless, it wasn't until a top executive at a much larger company, which was a supplier to Eric's firm, stopped in with one of his salesmen that things changed abruptly. "I was flabbergasted," said the executive. "Their operation was better than ours, and better than anyone else's, too." When the salesman told his boss, "No, they didn't clean up the place just for you. They didn't even know you were coming," the executive said, "We've got to have him," and two weeks later offered Eric $75,000 per year, a figure he thought was "probably only a little higher than Eric is making now." Four years later, Eric is earning $122,000 a year, and in the opinion of his boss, "saves us ten times what he costs us. And the place never ran smoother."

Similarly, Audrey made hand-knit apparel for nearly twenty-one years before anyone found her products "the hot new line." She had always had a few local customers, and some of the adventurous larger department stores took a few of her hats, scarves, and sweaters from time to time. But the amount of business she did barely covered her yarn bills.

With some regularity during those two decades, she talked of quitting, but it was clear she never meant it. "Maybe I should get a job at Jonathan Logan or Leslie Fay." But not only did she make no moves in that direction, she would not have accepted an offer had it been made.

Although on the surface nothing seemed to have changed from one decade to the next, buyers were slowly but surely coming to see both her and her work in a different light. Finally, one decided to take her seriously. "I decided to give her her own corner here," she said, "and see what happened." The order placed was much larger than anything Audrey had ever received before, more in fact than she could handle. She hired three people to help her, letting them know beforehand that they'd not get paid till she did.

As the buyer described what happened next, "The stuff just jumped off the rack." Audrey heard that with disbelief: "I'm glad. But I'm not doing *anything* different now than I've done for years." Nevertheless, her time had come, and once Audrey promised to expand, the store started taking full-page ads promoting her and her designs. She now employs fifty-one people and will do over $1.7 million worth of business this year.

In cases where the person was in the music, fiction writing, art or acting, sports or entertainment business, the curve was even more arced: often bouncing along the floor for a painfully long period and then suddenly shooting straight skyward. Not only did such people then make up for lost time, they made far more than they had imagined they would. One, a singer, who had been annoying her neighbors for years, began getting so many bookings she lamented, "There are now three of us in my act: me, my pianist, and Internal Revenue."

The wait always seemed long, even to those who'd not have chosen any other route. That they might be among the large majority in their field who will never make it was something they knew. But ignored. "I've tried other jobs," said one, "but I'm going to keep on sculpting until death or arthritis makes me stop." He won't have to worry. After years of just getting by, he is now earning more than he can spend. He was hooked, however, and was resigned to continue doing what he enjoyed, even if it never earned him a dime. Though it may be financially unfortunate for those who never succeed, that is apparently the kind of accidental dedication which is required.

QUESTION SIX. It sounds so gut-wrenching and soul-searing. What if I enjoy my work, but I'm not willing to crucify myself for it the way people who became rich did?

It might amuse you to know that neither were they. The Millionaire's Lie has an important, second part. Not only did those who eventually became wealthy hide how involved they were, they also hid the degree to which their work was easy—for them.

To see why they did so, let's go back to the prison yard. Suppose you, unlike the other prisoners, are not only getting paid and also enjoy your work, you in addition find it a breeze. All around you are angry convicts, sweating like pigs, trying hard to even do badly what you have little trouble doing well. Moreover, what takes them days to do you can accomplish in hours. And what they struggle with for hours you can casually do in minutes.

Again, the key question: Do you dare let them find that out?

If you are anything like the people we studied, you'd do the reverse. Those who eventually became wealthy learned how to grunt twice as loudly, instead. Their work was usually as easy for them as falling off the wall was for Humpty-Dumpty. But they gave—and still give—some of the finest theatrical performances to be seen anywhere. In an Academy Award-winning grimace, at a meeting one said he had worked for six hours on a marketing report that we knew had taken him all of ten minutes.

In a room full of liars, honesty may be the worst possible policy, so we're not suggesting he should have handled himself any differently. But as someone who eats, sleeps, and breathes the sales end of his company's business, he is turning a mole-hill into a mountain—one he hopes will match the size of the other mountain of complaints everyone else at the meeting showed up with.

The act, however, didn't end when the meeting did. Like the vast majority of people we studied, he made mountains out of molehills even when no one else was around. At first, that was puzzling. Why would people intentionally try to convince themselves their work is difficult when they know it isn't? Are they merely flattering themselves?

Sure, to some extent. But as it turns out, the main reason is that they don't want to think of themselves as liars. For safety's sake, they are used to presenting themselves to the other prisoners as being equally burdened. And they want to stick to that story even when alone: "Who, me? Easy? Hardly. I find my work as grueling as you find yours." That way, they don't have to worry about being found out.

Eliminating in this way the discrepancy between their pub-lic and private feelings helps prevent them from being caught with their guard down. But it also has the effect of killing some of the gleeful pleasure working would otherwise have for them.

Nor were they ready to drop that stance once the pressure of events made them public figures. They could, and did, then acknowledge how involved they were in their work. But they could not, and did not, let it be publicly known how easy they found their work. They still stayed with their Story of

Struggle, even though they knew as well as we did that it had been nothing of the sort. Horatio Alger's story, it turns out, is the saga of someone deathly afraid of the wrath of his fellow prisoners.

There are two main reasons why it was necessary for those who had become successful to continue with this deliberate falsehood, and in some cases expand it into a tear-jerking tale of bravery in the face of impossible odds. First, try telling someone that you do easily what they do only with great effort. How do you think they will react? Typically, they think you are boosting yourself up by putting them down. Not only are they likely to find your attempt to make yourself seem superior obnoxious, they may very well become hostile enough to try doing something about it—such as pointing out a weakness or inferiority you have which they don't.

Second, and of great importance, if they are paying you for a product you made or a service you render, they don't want to believe that you can produce or dispense it as easily as you blink. They want you instead to suffer and sweat a little in the process. Why? It is worth remembering that, particularly where the public is concerned, what they need most, and have come to you to buy, is your authenticity. Having put Stage Two first, they have lost theirs.

They thus want undeniable evidence that you have agonized over your work. How else could it have emerged from your darkest depths? Nothing is more convincing to them than to witness the event with their own eyes: to be present, to actually watch you groan and shake during your creative moments.

When Leo plays the piano before an audience, he always looks as if he is in pain. That is strange, because when playing the same piece at home the day before the concert, he played it relaxedly. Both performances were taped and are essentially identical, yet his facial and bodily gestures during the two were as different as day and night.

When asked about the gesturing, he replied, "I want to

communicate my feelings of ecstasy about the music." It is simply cheerleading, then, right? Not entirely, for if he played the piece as casually as he in fact can, no one would consider the performance truly authentic. And that, even more than the music, is what they have come for. He therefore forbids himself to smile while playing, fearful that someone might mistake him for Liberace. They want him to wriggle, writhe, and swoon, to prove his feelings run deep. So, without realizing why, he does.

So do millions of others, at work and at play. People in every profession, and at every position within the field, are trying to convince you that, as one put it, "I'm doing the best that I can." And another, "No one tries harder. My heart is really in it." And a third, "I always give it my all." Well, if you are "killing yourself, working like a slave every day," you are in the wrong field. No one who became a millionaire felt that way—until they had already become one.

In short: amazingly, the vast majority feel as if they are "getting away with something" when they do what they enjoy, get paid for it as well, and in addition find it easy to do. That view could hardly be more bizarre, or harmful. For when all is said and done, they are recoiling from the very trio of things they need most if they are to stand a good chance of achieving their lifelong dream of becoming rich.

QUESTION SEVEN. Abandoning the old pattern doesn't sound easy. How do I avoid being unwittingly influenced into taking a step backward by those around me?

The most important step is the first, and it calls for you to begin to recognize when someone is doing the false sweat, Horatio Humbug Alger or Millionaire's Lie routine for your benefit. One thing is certain: you won't have to wait very long for a practice opportunity to appear.

For instance, as long as we all insist on associating pain and achievement, Hollywood will give us exactly what we want. Using the worst and stiffest actors it can find, great achievements will be depicted as always being accompanied by great groans and grimaces. Every major accomplishment of mankind will be stuffed into a mold made of a mixture of Michelangelo's Sistine suffering, Beethoven's turmoil, and Van Gogh's distress. Needless to say, the farcically inflated depictions will subsequently be rehearsed everywhere by aspiring artists, writers, composers, musicians—and millionaires.

After you have seen enough people go through such knotted theatrics, their actions will strike you as merely hilarious, at best, and a bit idiotic, at worst. Yet it is worth reminding yourself at such moments what the underlying purpose of their behavior is: they don't want to be attacked. For that reason, they are prepared to go to unbelievable lengths to be believable. Theirs is a vastly overdone defense, one for which they are paying a much higher price than they realize.

Even among those who are vaguely aware that their own actions smack of fraud, many won't stop. They think that making mountains out of molehills helps. Basically, their justification is: "If I admit that the work is easy, I won't do it. I need the challenge." By giving themselves "an enormous problem to conquer," they hope to keep themselves interested in and focused upon it. For a few, it works. But the large majority will find that far too exhausting a route. And the odds are good that they will give up the fight long before their battle for fame and fortune has been won.

Not surprisingly, we are back to the topic of persistence. And the central question here is whether self-imposed obstacles and self-induced theatrical suffering are aiding—or preventing—you from getting what you want, and need. True, such actions help fend off attack. But at what cost?

There is indeed an easier way. It involves becoming comfortable with the second part of the Millionaire's Lie. Specifically, if you are being paid to do something you enjoy, and happen to do it easily as well, know it. Become comfortable with it. Admit it openly and unashamedly to yourself—though not to anyone else. We don't live in a world in which people rejoice in their work, and hence are glad that you enjoy yours. Quite the reverse; the majority don't like theirs, and expect you to suffer if you happen to be well rewarded for yours. ("He gets $200,000 a year," said one. "So what?" said the other contentedly. "Look how fast his job is making him age.")

That being the case, we need to be wary of anyone who tells us they do their work easily and well. It may, of course, be a mere statement of fact. But far more often it is a foolishly self-destructive comment. Animosity is easily aroused when most people see themselves as prisoners while the rest (who aren't) are trying hard to act as if they were.

In short: it was exceedingly rare for any of the people who eventually became millionaires to let anyone—including themselves—know how easily they did their work. Make one simple change: let yourself know. Accidental persistence is the name of the game. And nothing even comes close to generating as much of it as the realization that your work is satisfying, may one day make you rich and famous, and is easy, as well, at least for you.

QUESTION EIGHT. Suppose I admit that I usually find my work easy, and that I'm as good as the next person at making it seem hard. Are you suggesting that work I enjoy should never be difficult?

Not at all. Every line of work presents those who are doing it with certain difficulties. But the most important problem anyone who wants to become rich must solve is this: how are they going to "get into" their work in the first place? To put it bluntly: if you can become absorbed by your work day in and day out, for years on end, you'll get where you want to go, all right. In fact, it will be hard for anyone or anything to stop you.

Surprisingly, everyone had some difficulty getting into their work. But those who eventually became wealthy overcame that (very real) obstacle. However, and this is the critical point, it wasn't merely because they "tried harder." All that "shoulder to the wheel" and "nose to the grindstone" stuff turned out to be utter rubbish. The reason they found them-selves capable of repeatedly becoming absorbed by their work was that they found it deeply satisfying and were good at it.

If either of those factors was missing, the person simply did not persist. Bill, who initially thought he wanted to be an en-gineer, later developed some doubts. Although he had been well trained at one of the nation's best engineering schools and had done well throughout his undergraduate and graduate years, he began to feel the urge to write science fiction. "I'd always been an avid reader of sci-fi," he said, "and thought I could do better stories than the ones I was reading."

At the age of thirty-four, he had been working for nine years, and was liking it less each year than the one before. The pettiness of every electronics project in which he had a hand began to irritate him greatly. He has been writing sci-ence fiction stories for the last eight years, however, and al-though there is as much pettiness involved in the writing, typ-ing, photocopying, mailing, continuing conversation with his agent, and frustrating contact with potential publishers, he doesn't mind it in the least. Nor has the fact that none of his stories has yet been published dampened his enthusiasm.

He still works a forty-four-hour week at his firm, but man-ages to find the time to write. For that reason, he'll stay on, "and," he adds, "working here gives me a lot of good ideas." For all the engineering talent he possesses, he doesn't find his work sufficiently engrossing to, as he put it, "do it with more than my left hand."

Similarly, Betsy's linguistic skills are substantial. An English major in college, she found the first three jobs she held after graduation boring. A friend of hers, whom she had met in a French class in school, helped her land a position in which she could put her abilities to use. Nevertheless, Betsy felt outdis-tanced. "I was no match for her in school," she said of her friend's greater skills in this area, "and it was hard to keep up with her again, once we decided to learn Italian and Russian." They translated novels, short stories, and poetry. Although Betsy found the work fascinating, her friend did not and instead spent much of the time complaining about "all the trivia we are usually buried under."

They collaborated on a few ventures in the beginning, but it was interesting to see a shift slowly occurring as the years went by. Betsy was able to spend endless numbers of hours absorbed in the projects she had undertaken. Moreover, she consistently underestimated the amount of time she devoted to each. Her friend, on the other hand, resented every additional second a project required to complete beyond that which she had allotted to it. Within six years, it was no longer so clear who was outdistancing whom. Five years later Betsy translated a novel which became a best seller. A review in a major newspaper placed a good part of the responsibility for the book's success squarely in Betsy's lap. The reviewer went on to state that she thought the translation better written than the original.

You probably won't be surprised by now to hear that it was only after Betsy's earnings soared, and she began receiving a fair amount of publicity, that she started telling people how "backbreaking" an effort had been required to do a good job. It sounded odd. For except when her friend, the prisoner, had been around, and Betsy then felt compelled to produce a few complaints of her own, it was clear she found the work entrancing. On many an occasion, she had even called it fun.

In short, some people may be better than others at "getting into" their work on a particular day. But over a span of years, it is now clear that there is no such thing: those who were better at becoming absorbed by their work looked forward to being caught up in it and also found it inherently rewarding.

Ability alone simply won't do. We watched a large number of people repeatedly attempt to push themselves to do their work. As we've mentioned, a certain amount of focusing and initial self-coaxing was required by everyone. Few merely snapped their fingers and were off and running. Nonetheless, many never became absorbed by what they were doing. And their frustrating inability spawned many self-lectures about "giving it the old college try, again."

The experience millions have had in their student years proved to be the worst possible guide to what would be required of them later. "I hated Spanish," said one, "and I've managed to forget everything I learned. But I got through four semesters of it." It worked in college primarily because each course lasted only a matter of months, and although pushing yourself may be hard, it isn't something you have to do forever.

Unlike what happens in college, however, your work will last forty years, not four. Your mind automatically connects today's work to yesterday's and tomorrow's—particularly if you are not fond of what you are doing—to make your day seem interminable.

In sum, there are millions of people who are cheating their employer out of money, one paycheck at a time. But in the process, they are cheating themselves out of the possibility of making a fortune, and enjoying their lives, as well.

The pattern you established in school will do for you now what it did for you then: get you through short time-periods. The techniques you perfected will help you "get today out of the way." But they will never make you rich.

For that to happen, you need work which you find sufficiently absorbing to make older units of time—days, weeks, semesters, and academic years—blend into one another, enjoyably allowing your skills to develop without your being aware that they have. You won't have, nor do you want, quantitative measures of how well you are doing each week. For it is precisely the absence of exams, coupled with the magnetic appeal of the work itself, which will allow you to do far more than you ever would have in school.

QUESTION NINE. Instead of worrying about it at all, why don't I just marry someone who is already rich?

That is harder to do than you might imagine, and becoming increasingly so. Over the last two decades, the people we studied have expressed a growing concern that their prospective

partner have approximately the same amount of money as
they. That wasn't so in the 1960s, an aggressively egalitarian
and prosperous period, when many felt uncomfortable about
even having, much less expressing, a preference for a partner
whose assets and earnings matched their own.

The end of the decade marked a major turning point. The
recession which occurred in 1970 brought an abrupt halt to
the lack of concern about the subject. Whereas in not one of
the nine previous years did more than 21 percent express a
preference at all, with a record low of 9 percent doing so in
1968, by 1971 the proportion of people expressing one jumped
to over 49 percent. In less than twenty months—from February 1969 to September 1970—the prevailing indifference was
dealt a surprisingly severe blow. Subsequently, in every year
except 1973 the percentage continued to increase.

In general, when times were good and the economy was
doing well, people gave the matter less thought. But when
economic conditions deteriorated, the income and wealth of
their potential partner once again became important. "I don't
want to have to support someone else," said one. "I'm barely
able to support myself right now." Another commented, "If I
hook up with someone with a lot less money than me, we'll be
in a bind." In 1974, a poor year economically, the proportion
rose above 70 percent for the first time.

One year, 1979, was unique. It was the only one in which
the index of concern increased substantially, even though the
economy also continued to grow. The outbreak of a rash of
lawsuits by live-in lovers was responsible for the rise. What
the suits succeeded in doing was to accelerate a steady trend
which had been well under way for a decade.

It also freed the trend from its dependence on the business
cycle. If you had money, you could be sued during both bad
times and good. The fact that economic conditions had im-
proved to a point where people were feeling somewhat more
optimistic about the economic outlook wasn't likely to deter
them from trying to enjoy the good times even more, with
your money.

What needs to be added immediately is that our preferences and reality often don't match. What we'd like to have happen and what does frequently have little in common. That is particularly so where meeting "an ideal partner" is concerned. Even if we could accurately describe the person with whom we'd be happiest, running across the person under the right circumstances is another matter entirely.

The people we studied tended to choose partners from among their co-workers and those they met during leisure activities they enjoyed. Their partner's financial status usually was overlooked in the heat of the moment. If they and the person "clicked," the issue wound up being temporarily forgotten, surfacing again later only after the two had been together awhile.

For some, however, it was never forgotten, not even in the first few minutes or meetings. They were openly in search of a wealthy partner, and had no intention of tying up with someone who wasn't very well off. They were convinced that the best and straightest road to riches was the social one, and hence in every sense, their socializing was a business. They knew that as long as they kept partying and going through a series of partners, their work was temporary employment, a series of short-term jobs. They didn't want it to continue that way forever. Their intention was to find permanent employment as soon as possible by marrying someone rich.

Much to their distress, if they got what they wanted, they typically found their work never ended. Whenever they needed money, they had to get some from their partner. It was still a series of brief jobs. But this time, instead of selling themselves to a sequence of social employers, there was only one who had to be sold—or should we say "conned"?—repeatedly. That could become incredibly tiring. "The money was good," said one, who although penniless had managed to marry someone who stood to inherit $12 million, "but I got tired of waiting for the 'big stuff' to arrive." Latching onto someone wealthy obviously wasn't the same as finding a winning million-dollar lottery ticket: the money you won in the lottery was yours to do with as you pleased. Your partner's money, on the other hand, always came with your partner attached, something which in time might prove unbearably irritating.

When all is said and done, what is wrong with looking for a potential partner who is rich is that it requires you to put Stage Two first. Your financial goals are given priority over finding a field you enjoy. You probably won't be surprised to hear that pairing up with someone rich—and bearable—proved as hard for the people we studied as finding the spectacularly successful investments most sought. Many, in fact, spent the entire twenty-year period looking for a monied mate. Unfortunately, they have paid the same price everyone with Stage Two first has: they haven't located the pot of gold at the end of the rainbow, and in the process, they have annoyingly wasted two decades trying.

QUESTION TEN. As I see it, the next best thing to marrying someone wealthy is to become a dentist, lawyer, accountant, or especially, a doctor. Those people automatically become rich, don't they?

No, and we were as surprised at that as you probably are. Everything seemed all right in Stage One. The area they had chosen to study certainly seemed to interest them. Actually, it had to. For example, the training of a physician lasts long enough so that medical students with little interest in the field of medicine would have found the huge number of hours they had to devote to the subject intolerable.

Also, once they finished their training, it was easier for them to remain involved in their work, because their day usually consisted of talking to people. One, who had just finished telling us he had grown tired of his specialty, which was pediatrics, became actively involved again in a flash, once his next patient arrived and began describing a complaint.

People who work at a desk in an office, on the other hand, may find it more difficult to keep themselves involved. No one is standing right in front of them with a personal or medical problem serious enough to have brought the person there in the first place, one which the person is even willing to pay to get help in solving.

Where professionals got themselves in trouble with astonishing frequency was in the Stage Two aspects of their lives. They were the worst investors we studied.

Their professional training has lasted for so many years, during which time they had earned little or nothing, they completed their period of study with a pent-up hunger for money. "Now," one who had just finished his surgery residency said, "I'm going to make up for lost time."

There was also a widespread desire among the professionals we studied to "get even with the public." You won't like the way it sounds. They weren't all that happy with their own thoughts here, either. But it is what they felt, and strongly, at that. "My training has been very long and very expensive. The only reason it was is so that I can be exceptionally well qualified to treat your ills. Well, I hated having it cost so much and take so long. And now you—each and every one of you—is going to make it up to me by paying through the nose."

It wasn't an all-consuming passion for each. But most were indeed in a hurry to become wealthy. It was almost as if, having had to put Stage One first and stay involved with their work for many years, they were now going to put Stage Two first, with a vengeance.

Not all their reasons for doing so were financial. As diligent students, ones who had spent many more years in school than the majority of their friends, they felt "out of it." And since, in addition, the legal, financial, or medical material they had to learn was more difficult than the subjects most of their high school classmates had chosen to study, they felt bookish and too serious. Now, however, they were going to be *cool*. As one put it, "With money, I'll be like everybody else." As they saw it, by putting Stage Two first, they were at last going to enter the social mainstream.

Also, they honestly thought the attitude would make them rich. Could all their peers, almost all of whom strongly believed in Stage Two first, be wrong? As one, a young lawyer, put it two years after completing law school, "To make big money, you have to *concentrate* on making big money." It sounds so obvious, it would have been difficult to argue with. But it's wildly inaccurate, anyway. In fact, the reverse was the case. Particularly in the professions, the ones who eventually made the most by far were those who loved their work the most.

Professionals who put Stage Two first had the same thing happen to them that happened to others with a similarly upside-down set of priorities: they wound up losing interest in their field. And because after graduation professionals pursued wealth with such secret ferocity, they lost interest more rapidly than most. Their bitterness in time grew to substantial proportions. It was well grounded, in any event. After all, they hadn't become rich, and they found their work increasingly annoying, as well.

The main reason they hadn't yet become wealthy was because the substantial sums they earned working they invested with an incompetence that is hard to believe. Some people think of pill-pushing physicians as being much like snake oil salesmen. However, the physicians we studied were more likely to buy the stuff than sell it. They didn't actually purchase any, of course. But they did buy just about everything else, including a "fabulous homesite" in Florida which was indeed under water. The broker seems to have neglected to mention who would be "at home" there.

Rather than reviewing the long list of half-baked schemes which consumed their capital, the matter can be summarized simply: anything anyone tried to sell them which sounded at all reasonable as an "investment"—a magic word—they bought. Their speculative purchases differed little from those made by others. But they had far more money to use for the purpose, so they managed to buy every "investment" available, from the reasonable to the ridiculous. Thanks to their hurry, the emphasis was usually on the latter.

It was probably unrealistic to think, as we originally did, that they would fare better than the average investor. Yet we were surprised to see them do so much worse. What needs to be emphasized here, however, is that they couldn't reinvest in themselves the sizable sums they earned annually.

The professions are unique in that respect. They require a great deal of money to be spent "up front." Anyone wanting to enter the professions must make a major investment in schooling, in order to enter the field at all. But having done that, the money they subsequently make, and don't use for daily living expenses, typically has no place to go except in search of investments.

The financial lives of professionals thus soon developed a split personality. On the one hand, they felt pressure to live well, both to make up for the long, hard times as a student and because it was an appropriate part of the image they wanted to project. On the other hand, they worried continually about increasing the capital they had accumulated. The public spending and picture of comfort contrasted sharply with a private tendency to hoard money and invest it hurriedly.

A carpenter-turned-cabinetmaker we followed had no similar difficulties. He reinvested almost all his earnings in his expanding business. And the firm's profits as well were invested in the same way. Professionals normally have nothing comparable available to them. In short, the professions may offer more prestige, but its members are prevented from having investment opportunities be an integral part of their practice. Their frenzied search for places to park their investment capital is largely inevitable.

The last straw, the one which literally broke the camel's back, was the fact that most professionals—particularly dentists and doctors—have no business experience. "Why," you might ask, "don't they go get some? They have a large and growing amount of money to look after." The answer professionals give is a very good one. "It doesn't make sense for me to spend my time that way," they say, "because if I don't work, I don't earn."

They are in the business of selling their labor. Services, not products. Taking time away from their business to learn how to make money on their money costs them money. And the one thing most felt was that, above all, they had to concentrate on keeping their flow of income coming.

Besides, they knew how to do their work well enough to earn a decent living doing it. They weren't so sure they would ever make comparable amounts investing. As one put it, "I think I should stick with what I know." Their doubts were justified. But that didn't stop them from trying, anyway —and thanks to the fervor with which they had put Stage Two first, usually doing it badly.

QUESTION ELEVEN. You haven't mentioned marriage or the effect intimate personal relationships had on the outcome. Won't finding the right partner help me become rich?

We had hoped to find a high correlation between certain kinds of romantic pairings and success. There wasn't any. Finding the right partner won't help you significantly to become wealthy. And conversely, tying up with the wrong one isn't likely to significantly harm your chances, either.

Like most others, we at first believed the comments people made attributing their success—or failure—to their partners. "I couldn't have done it without her," one said. "He made it all possible," said another. The same, when things went badly: "He was the one who stopped me from succeeding," and, "I'd have made it big if it hadn't been for her."

The comments turned out to be rubbish. When things go well for us, we don't want to be accused of bragging. So we willingly share the stage. And when we flop, it is wonderfully easy and convenient to blame it all on whoever happens to be closest to us at the time.

Over an extended period it became clear, however, that the

more someone was used to blaming their own failures on others, the more likely they were to keep on doing just that once they teamed up with someone else. The partner no more "caused" the present failures than the past ones. The only constant was the tradition of blame, which continued before, during, and after the partner was a part of their lives.

It was a costly tradition. People who were inclined to dump the responsibility for failure on an intimate were significantly less likely to eventually become wealthy. The reason why didn't take long to discover: sooner or later, they wound up doing the same thing at work they were doing at home. And while it may have been hard for an intimate to draw a dividing line and determine to what extent each was at fault, coworkers had no such difficulty. They had none of the inclination lovers often evidence to accept blame they didn't deserve, in order to keep the relationship going. Realizing that their jobs were on the line, they in fact were just as happy to tell you to "stuff it" and reject all responsibility for failure even if they knew they had played a small role in producing it.

Be that as it may, there was a temptation on the part of many couples to go into business together. If you are thinking of doing something comparable, but haven't yet, let us offer a word of advice: Don't. In our sample, the chances of two people who were a couple as well as full-time business partners eventually being divorced from one another was more than two and a half times greater than when both were in different businesses.

Their fighting was usually sporadic at first, but rapidly became chronic. Arguments which ordinarily would have been forgotten widened into conflict about everything, and nothing. The business which was supposed to provide additional glue to keep the couple happily intertwined instead became an impediment to personal expression and soon was deeply resented. Not only did the relationship suffer, so did the business. They had teamed up with wealth as well as romance on their minds and wound up having neither. Each blamed the other, for both failures.

Whether or not the two were in business together, the fights couples had about money were one of the most absurd pieces of behavior we studied. That money was a common subject of dispute didn't make the fights about it any the less ludicrous. Each party insisted that their approach to financial matters was "best" and their way of thinking about money was "the right one."

Yet the fact remains that each of the three spending styles discussed in Chapter Two is merely different from, not better or worse than, the other two. High Rollers spent freely and easily, Low Rollers deliberated moderately about their purchases, while No Rollers agonized endlessly.

However, and this is crucial, there was no correlation between the degree to which someone agonized during a purchase and how wealthy they eventually became. Some were tightfisted beyond belief and still managed to become millionaires. (Their pinchpenny habits did at times embarrass their wealthy friends, one of whom only half jokingly said, "You're giving us all a bad name.") Others who became equally rich were as loose as a goose, and didn't spend a total of five minutes worrying about everything they bought during the twenty years.

Even though each spending style, from High through Low to No Roller, proved as effective as the others in making someone rich, what do you imagine happened when people with greatly differing spending styles paired up? It wasn't exactly what you'd call harmony. The fights they had were often heated enough to blister the paint off the walls—and were totally fruitless. Because this is one area of our personality which is very resistant to change. The amount of agonizing we do when making a purchase, rather than being an isolated aspect of who we are, is connected to everything we do, including our work and way of judging others.

Asking your partner to change in this area is much the same as asking him or her to find a new brain. Even if they could do as you ask, you might be surprised to see how many other facets of your relationship also changed once this one did. But there is no reason to change. Our lives aren't a bunch of little bits and pieces, habits and inclinations, which are unrelated. There is a unity to our behavior others can see, even if we can't. And especially over the long term, the way we conduct ourselves in one sphere has an important—and unbreakable—relationship to what we do in another.

Respecting the enormous number of individual differences which make us each unique probably won't, in and of itself, make you significantly richer. But it will make you happier while you are getting wherever you are going.

QUESTION TWELVE. There are more than six hundred books currently in print telling people how to "get rich quick." If I buy some—or all—of them, won't I get some good advice?

No. In fact, such books will make it harder, not easier, for you to ever become wealthy. For they all make the same fatal mistake: they encourage you to put Stage Two first. Many even go so far as to tell you to throw Stage One out altogether and concentrate instead on making money.

While some of the books are outright frauds, the rest of the authors simply haven't bothered to examine the evidence. The fact remains that the overwhelming majority of people who have become wealthy have become so thanks to work they found profoundly absorbing. And anyone who tells you to de-emphasize, much less discard, your work and attempt to directly seize fame and fortune is misleading you terribly, whether they are doing so intentionally or unintentionally.

The authors may themselves have been misled by the fact that, as we've seen repeatedly, people who have become rich do indeed appear to have "stumbled" into it. They were doing one thing, and suddenly, by doing another, they became millionaires. If the events which actually brought them their wealth are stripped of context and viewed in isolation, it might well appear that since those people just stumbled into a fortune, you can too.

Yet, the long-term study of people who eventually became

wealthy clearly reveals that their "luck" arose from the accidental dedication they had to an area they enjoyed. In fact, had they read the "get rich quick" books and followed the advice they found there, they would never have become rich to begin with.

All the books do is raise the odds against you—anything which encourages you to put Stage Two first does. The most avid readers of "get rich quick" books turned out to be the least successful people we studied. That is, until they stopped reading the books, forgot the "foolproof" schemes, and concentrated instead on work they found absorbing. You should be doing the same.

QUESTION THIRTEEN. What you say in Chapter Ten about de-emphasizing competitiveness and concentrating instead on work I enjoy sounds fine, but my boss keeps insisting that we must "stay competitive." How am I supposed to do both?

Easily. The phrase "stay competitive" was the source of a substantial amount of confusion in the minds of the people we studied. Put simply: *you* don't have to be competitive for your firm to be. What is true for companies need not—and, our results indicate, should not—be true for the employees working at them. A firm that intends to remain free of the wasteful effects of excessive in-house rivalry needs to select the right employees. Those who enjoy what they're doing will help the firm maintain *its* competitive position, a necessity. They'll do it not so much by snarling at the enemy, but by going about their business, each doing the work he or she finds most satisfying.

That doesn't mean every bright idea developed by people who are absorbed in their work will be commercial. It may be an idea whose time hasn't yet arrived, or one whose time has already come and gone. It also might be too expensive to implement. Whatever the case, that type of thinking and the deep involvement required to come up with it in the first place are what is needed to allow any company to "stay competitive" in every department, from development and production to sales and distribution.

Without it, the firm must scramble to cover itself every time another company introduces something new. At some point, it has to start coming up with its own ideas and directions rather than being continually jerked all over the map by its competitors.

Granted, going your own way at first glance seems to be enormously more of a gamble than is copying what has already succeeded. But the evidence here is unequivocal. Copying may earn you a living, but only work you enjoy will make you rich.

Imitating what produced a huge profit for someone else may not even prove profitable for you. Although it is commonly assumed that copying what others have made fortunes from will always make money for you, the facts simply don't bear that out. And the reason why is clear: there is only one original, but there are lots of copies. You won't be the only one in the business of imitating something which has already become a hit. And while you're doing so, whoever it was that produced the original to begin with will be getting yet another step ahead of you. It is a hard and frustrating dollar to earn, if you make it at all.

We found that the majority of executives who compulsively devoted themselves to "keeping up" with what was going on at other firms, and who expected their employees to do the same, produced pervasive anxiety, not profits. In essence, they were squandering the company's most precious asset, the time and talents of its best people. Deathly afraid of losing, such executives drafted their subordinates into an army devoted to fending off the enemy. It had a ring of rationality to it ("We have to keep up with what others are doing"), and so even though the employees had been involuntarily conscripted into a military campaign to defend their leader against his own fears, they went along with it.

What they didn't know was that they were involved in a permanent war, which their side could only lose. By managing to maintain the appearance of keeping up, they thought they were helping their company to at least break even, and that the intercompany conflict was a stalemate. Yet, without realizing it, they were sustaining a major loss. The only way they could have gotten a big jump on the enemy was to concentrate on the areas of their work which they enjoyed—the very thing the atmosphere of intense competitiveness guaranteed they would be unable to do.

QUESTION FOURTEEN. To tell you the truth, it's not only my boss. I also am very competitive. What can I do about it?

So is everybody else—primarily when other competitive people are around. And the only remedy that really works is this: stop competing *continually*.

In the U.S. the emphasis is on winning and how to be a good winner. "Show your sportsmanship" and "be humble," you are told. No one tells you that there will be defeats as well as victories, and hence that it is important for you to learn how to handle a setback.

What is so ironic about the situation is that what looks like a loss may be the very event which is subsequently responsible for helping to produce the major achievements of your life. With our extreme emphasis on winning, when something good happens to us, we look to thank the people who we think helped us. What we don't say is, "Thanks to so-and-so for firing me from a job which would have led me to dribble my life away on empty, if prestigious and well-paid, nonsense." We express our gratitude to the people we like for their encouragement, and not to the people we loathe for their no less valuable efforts to discourage us. Strange as it may sound to ears used to hearing nothing but the noise of victory celebrations, sometimes your enemies are more valuable than your friends in preventing you from speeding toward what, for you, would have been a dead end.

Specifically, what is required is to exchange many small, short-term losses for one large, long-term gain. If life is viewed as a fight with 150 rounds in it and you aren't going to allow yourself to lose even one of the 150, you won't win the fight. Because the difference between a professional boxing match and what happens to you where your work is concerned is that, in reality, you can make any one of those rounds last as long as you like. It's easy to convert a three-minute round into a thirty-year battle.

Why do you imagine anyone would do such a thing? The reason is that they are losing, of course. And they don't want to lose. God, if you only knew how much they don't want to lose. So Round Seventeen, say, lasts thirty years, since as long as it continues, they don't have to accept the verdict. As a result, there is no eighteenth round, or nineteenth. Unfortunately for them, they weren't going to start winning big until they got to the 106th round, and they never got anywhere near it.

It has nothing to do with fate. But in this boxing match, you begin Round One with no well-developed skills at all. Just a lot of potential. You've never boxed before, and the way the sport is structured, you can learn only by doing. Yet you somehow became convinced that you were never supposed to lose. Ever. People who feel that way will spend their lives redoing one galling round they didn't win.

What is hard for them to recognize is that they cannot win it, no matter how many decades they devote to it. For their opponent would rather die than lose. No matter how far they are prepared to go, their opponent is willing to go—in fact, must go—a step further. To the person in the opposite corner, losing is the same as dying.

There is one other, strange aspect of the boxing match into which your work automatically throws you: in each round, you will face a new partner. But if you stay in one round, stuck there by your need to defeat someone who appears to have handed you a loss, then and only then does the fight become much like an ordinary boxing match.

Had you gotten on with the fight and allowed the other rounds to come and go, doing the best you could in each, your skills would slowly have developed substantially—even if you were among the last to realize it. Had that happened, you would have been stunned to see that in the later rounds some of your opponents might have admired you sufficiently to not only let you win, but also to want to help you win the remaining rounds.

Only "win some, lose some," instead of "win every one," will ever allow that to happen. But it will remain superficial and useless advice unless you realize that the "losses" you sustain are setting the stage for the very things you want most to have happen to you. In short, the conclusion is inescapable: if you never learn to accept a loss, that is what your entire life will end up being.

Paradoxically, those who feel compelled to compete continually find themselves losing more often, not less. They are viciously competitive in an enormous number of situations which simply don't require it, since nothing of real importance is at stake. Constant competitiveness, rather than masking inferiority feelings, serves only to highlight them instead.

QUESTION FIFTEEN. There is often a lot of envy and anger mixed in with my competitive feelings. When someone obnoxious bumps me out of the way and succeeds in getting ahead as a result, I get very annoyed. What am I supposed to do with all those feelings, forget them?

Hardly. They are normal, and almost inevitable under the circumstances. More than 73 percent of the people we studied answered "Yes", when we asked them, "Have you ever felt like killing a competitor of yours?"

The answers to "When?" varied. Some said, "In traffic." Others said, "On line at the bank, supermarket, or fast-food counter," etc. Nevertheless, the really deep hatred was reserved for their rivals at work. Unlike what occurred at the bank or supermarket, the situation at the office often became critical, for rather than being an isolated event, which was over in a matter of minutes, it went on for weeks, months, or even years. Some said they would have liked nothing better than to hire a "hit man" to remove their odious adversary.

The key question here is: How sensible would it be for you to get into a fistfight with someone who cuts in front of you at the bank or store? We're not suggesting you turn the other cheek; if you can do something about the rude intruder, do it. But not at the expense of your life or limbs. Remember, you may be dealing with a certified nut. A genuinely insane individual. In that case, the confrontation can easily get out of hand, and if it does, quite apart from any harm which befalls you, you may find when it's over that you forgot to do your banking or shopping. In the heat of the conflict, your purpose for being there to begin with may be overlooked.

The same applies to what happens to you in a similar situation at work. If your mind is feverishly occupied with when and how you are going to vent your anger upon someone who may well deserve it for the way they treated you, you are likely to overlook your purpose in being there to begin with. The difficulty is that this time you won't notice it. Your trip to the bank or supermarket was for something specific, and any hostile encounter you have while there isn't likely to make you forget what it was.

That is not so where your work is concerned. We found that most people, when antagonized, were distracted substantially from pursuing the tasks they wanted to accomplish. Some even forgot in the process why they had come to the office at all.

The best reason not to fight with the crazies you encounter either publicly or privately is that sooner or later, someone else will do it for you. Someone equally crazy, in fact. They will be a good match for one another. And with any luck, they might even do each other in.

Oddly enough, that is also the best reason for not becoming endlessly entangled with someone who is obnoxiously competitive at work. Sooner or later, they too are going to encounter someone just like themselves. In fact, they will be drawn to one another, because both speak the same language and no one else wants either of them around. Instead of wasting many days which could be put to better use doing what you want to accomplish, let someone else exact your revenge for you.

It is indeed irksome to let them go. But even though they have gotten ahead of you, they aren't going very far. The chances are good that at best, they will move into the Middle Management Asteroid Belt and go no further. Surrounded by people equally if not more malicious than they, they will suddenly be seen for what they are. As it turns out, the world does a far better job of getting even with such viciously competitive people for you than you can.

It may not be a very consoling fact—but it is a fact, nonetheless—that the most miserable and obnoxious people we studied usually had to rise a notch before they could be stopped. In scores of instances, what typically happened was that they stole credit from someone and were promoted. Then they stole it again and were fired.

Vent the angry feelings through regular exercise, help get the person fired if you can do so without much effort, and spend your time and energy on the areas you enjoy. If you do, you will be pleasantly surprised to see who ultimately comes out ahead.

CHAPTER THIRTEEN

How Will You Get There?—
The Only Strategy
That Really Works

QUESTION SIXTEEN. How, step by step, do I go about getting there?

Everything we discuss in this chapter can be described as "shaping your work." It is more malleable than clay, and needs to be molded if it is to stand a good chance of helping to make you rich.

There are two principal dimensions: What you do, and whom you do it with? As you'll see shortly, we need to look at the second aspect first.

In certain ways, it would be nice if we were all insensitive and when we wanted to do something (assuming it wasn't destructive) we just went ahead and did it. Usually, what prevents us from just plunging ahead is the people we know.

Those around us affect us. And they do so far more than most of us would care to admit. What is important about that for our purposes is this: working closely with people you don't like will prevent you from being involved with your work, and hence will block the best road you have open to you, if you are ever to find fame or fortune.

To see why, think about what happens to you when you are watching a movie you find very absorbing. If someone a few seats away starts talking loudly, then instead of being able to ignore them and stay happily involved with what you were watching you'll "snap out of it." And be annoyed. They are taking something precious from you.

That is much more so at work, where people who annoy and interfere may end up costing you a small fortune. You are unlikely to be in the same semihypnotic state you are in a movie theater, but the differences here are much less than had previously been thought. Those who eventually became rich were absorbed by their work repeatedly, and for prolonged periods. And when they were, they were even more lost to the world than they'd have been while watching a movie.

The two events seem more different than they actually are, because in business, you are frequently talking, whereas in a theater, you are silent. Also, in an office, the lights are on and you are either interacting with the people around you or at any moment may have to. In the theater, the lights are out and the people around you matter little.

Yet the similarities between the two events are enormously more important than the differences. People who have spent years absorbed in their work finally develop the phenomenal ability to talk without rupturing their connection to their thoughts. They are absorbed "on the run," as opposed to someone who is doing the same while seated passively in a theater. They have learned how to go through the motions of being sociable and cooperative, but through it all maintain a high state of involvement with their work.

Business executives who shook their heads in mock puzzlement at Einstein's deep involvement in his work were no less involved with theirs. The difference is that they had the ability to talk (to someone else) while continuing to think, whereas mathematicians and physicists often concentrate silently (or talk to themselves).

People in business thus unwittingly exaggerate the difference between the two groups. After all, hardheaded executives, responsible for money, products, and people, would hardly feel comfortable about being accused of "talking to themselves." So they aim their thoughts at others, make it look like conversation, and thus give the appearance of being, by their standards, normal. Since they think best aloud anyway, the process works well for them.

Three things make being absorbed crucial. First, it makes time fly. If you want to see how long eight hours can be, try doing something you dislike for that entire time. On the other hand, an activity you find absorbing shrinks time, often making hours seem like minutes. The second reason, then, is that your skills will develop more rapidly. Since you are unaware of how much time is passing, you put in more of it. Third, you don't notice the time, but you will notice the contentment. There is something inherently satisfying about being absorbed, whether it be by a person or project you love. Having experienced it once, you'll want to do so again. And again.

We aren't talking about trances and mystical states which require catch phrases, repeated endlessly, or drugs to induce. The state of absorption we're referring to is something everyone has experienced at one time or another. And what typically induced it was something they were reading, listening to, or watching.

It feels good. But business people in particular are uncomfortable with the concept. Many said, "Only dope addicts get like that." The comment reveals a fundamental misunderstanding. Contrary to what they have been led to believe, there are two kinds of involvement: passive *and* active absorption. Sitting stumplike, in a trance, cross-eyed and immobile, is an example of the former. Having sex is an example of the latter.

In short, people who eventually became millionaires repeatedly got "stoned on their work." Rather than being rigid and still, however, they were occasionally in a state of frenzy, as plans and ideas came pouring out of them. Their behavior stood in stark contrast to that of people who found no area of work fascinating and hence who (wanting equally to be involved) produced a useless high, thanks to chants and chemicals. The need to be absorbed was there, but work wasn't used to fulfill it.

The long-term effects on the lives of people in the two groups were vast. Those using drugs to stay high·were as passive as rocks, literally could be described as stoned, and not surprisingly, went nowhere. Those who were absorbed by their work learned more and then earned more. Theirs was an immensely productive high.

People who were actively absorbed in their work did occasionally make use of drugs, trances, and alcohol as a means of temporarily relaxing. But they were unhappy being passive and unproductive for long, and thus willingly returned to the captivating area of activity they enjoyed. You can call what they were doing "work"; they knew only that it was satisfying. It often seemed more like play.

What makes the people you work closely with so important is that they are in a position to sever your connection to your work. If you are required to function side by side with a person you loathe, someone who upsets and annoys you, something very destructive happens. Some of that hatred will spill over from your attitude toward the person and contaminate your attitude toward your work.

Keeping the two separate is apparently quite difficult. And with good reason, as we saw in the example of what happens to you at the movies. Once the person has succeeded in interrupting your involvement with your work, much of what made your work appealing to you to begin with will be gone. In an important sense, you do indeed come to like your work less, thanks to the interference.

If the intrusion is brief and you are hindered only temporarily from getting back into your work, no harm is usually done. But in a large number of instances, the intruders weren't about to leave. For they too were being paid to be present.

What is necessary, in sum, is to protect your relationship to your work. That sounds somewhat fastidious or priggish, but it is intended to convey a simple fact: those who were pestered by a co-worker, and whose state of active absorption was halted as a result, soon became disenchanted with their work if the interference continued for any length of time.

In an appalling number of cases, people came to the conclusion they hated their work, as well as their co-workers. That may have been so, in some instances. But in many others, it was fascinating to see that once the intruder was removed or left, the state of contented absorption returned.

Step One, therefore, calls for you to be more selective when it comes to the people you work with. Of course, that is easier said than done. Your job probably requires you to interact with certain people in other slots, and coordinating your work with theirs necessitates contact with them. Nevertheless, any progress you can make in this area has generally proved itself invaluable.

The major reason most of the people we studied did not attempt to limit their contact with an obnoxiously competitive or hostile co-worker was fear of offending the person. If only a few people had been so thoughtful and polite to someone who was malicious, the problem would have been a minor one. But excessively considerate behavior was displayed by a majority. They did not respond promptly or effectively when someone started making their lives miserable. Instead, they reacted slowly and belatedly, if at all. In many instances, they never allowed their feelings of anger and annoyance to come to the surface.

To repeat what we said in an earlier chapter: this isn't a book on business etiquette. You have to decide what feels right to you and act accordingly. But consider the evidence: if someone at work irritates you continually, the odds are high that you will in time lose interest in your work because you can't get "into" it. It will be just a set of boring tasks, instead of a satisfyingly absorbing activity.

It is worth remembering, then, that a little bit of unpleasantness goes a long way. If someone is chronically nasty, no one will be surprised should they again be the same way. But you probably don't appear to be a snarling animal (even if there are days when you feel like one), and hence a harsh word or comment from you may have a significantly greater impact than it would from someone who is usually hostile. You have to be the judge, but anything that works to rid you of someone who is a constant nuisance is worthwhile.

The most shocking reason people who were being pestered gave us for not doing something about it was, "I won't get ahead if I do," and, "People will think I'm a troublemaker." By not offending people who are offending you, you can continue to hope that you'll win their vote in the office popularity contest. You may well be successful in getting them to think you are nice, even though you find them awful. However, when all is said and done, you will literally have won the battle and lost the war. Or won the round but lost the fight. Because in the long term, you'll pay the price if they rupture your involvement with your work—a highly probable outcome.

Your feelings about your co-workers will be clearer if you list the names of the ones you have frequent contact with. Next to each put a number, ranging from +10 for ones you very much enjoy working with to —10 for the ones you can't stand. Assigning a numerical value to each is something you'll probably have to do four or five times, over a period of weeks, since your opinion of them may change, particularly if you haven't yet come to know some of them very well.

In our study, people who rated their co-workers on average at +3.6 or better stood a significantly better chance of staying happily absorbed in—and hence accidentally persisting at—their work. You can, and should, attempt to raise your co-worker rating by "eliminating the negative": that is, start making a point of avoiding the people who received scores of —1 to —10, particularly those at or near the bottom of the range.

No one is suggesting you suddenly become the office bastard, loudly telling anyone who annoys you to "back off." It's easy to overdo it, once you get started. But putting a bit of distance between you and someone who is viciously competitive is very important, and will in all likelihood require you to offend them mildly. Although you may think you need a "good word" from them, you don't. The good opinion of someone that competitive too easily disappears, no matter how long and hard you worked to win it.

In fact, the thought: "What will happen if my co-workers don't like me?" turned out to be one of the most exaggerated fears the people we studied had. Everyone wants to be loved for themselves alone, not the particular skills they possess. But especially in a work context, people often value you in the long run precisely because you do your work well. And if you worry enough about what your co-workers think of you now, you might not be around later to see what they think of you.

Having discussed the people you work with, we turn now to the work itself. Very few of the people we studied liked every part of their jobs. Some aspects interested them greatly, others bored them to tears. What was puzzling, though, was how little they did to modify the situation. It made some sense that they didn't want to tell an obnoxious co-worker to leave them alone. But ridding themselves of the more obnoxious parts of their jobs would not have required a similarly continuing confrontation with a co-worker. Still, they did nothing about it.

There was some justification for the silence. The fact that people found only a portion of their work satisfying didn't serve to prevent them from persisting at it. The appealing parts obviously made up for the more appalling parts, and somehow most people continued doing both, more or less happily. Nevertheless, it was neither a necessary nor desirable condition.

Step Two, thus, calls for you to make a list of the major aspects of your job and put a number, ranging as before from

—10 to +10, next to each. Your attitude toward your work as a whole, much less each of its parts, will vary considerably from one day to the next. So once again, a series of ratings over an extended period of time is needed. However, most of the people we studied knew which parts of their work they enjoyed and which they'd have been happy to be rid of. Those who, on average, rated their work at +3.9 or higher persisted at it longer.

As before, "eliminating the negative" is the goal. It seems not to have occurred to most of the people in our sample that the activities they disliked someone else might have been thrilled to do. And vice versa. They simply accepted—as given—the job they held, rather than discussing with their boss a swapping away of the parts they found onerous in exchange for tasks they found more exciting.

It is extremely helpful, however, to "shape" your work, not only by being more selective about the people with whom you have regular contact but also by paring away the parts you find unpleasant. Often, a minor revision in both the people and parts made a major difference.

It is probably not a good idea to dispense with every last area you dislike, since something you have to do—but don't like doing—provides good grounds for an occasional groan. No matter how much those who eventually became millionaires enjoyed their work, from time to time they did love complaining about it. They bounced back and forth between periods when they were highly absorbed, and attended to a host of petty details without realizing it, and periods when they were restless and impatient, and made frustration-filled comments such as, "I just want something *big* to finally happen."

The former was progress, the latter was the person spinning his or her wheels. An excess of the latter merely resulted in a deep rut. If there was enough of the former, however, the destination was eventually reached. No one is perfect, though, and everyone who profoundly enjoyed their work also occasionally bitched.

Our focus thus far has been on what you do for a living and whom you do it with, because spending more of your workday in the company of people you like and concentrating on areas you enjoy will significantly improve your chances of becoming wealthy. As initial steps, you may thus have to consider changing your work and co-workers, not your job. Some minor modifications, and a few major ones as well, may be needed in order to make it more satisfying. It is less difficult to do than you might imagine, and is worth trying.

However, if you remain discontent in spite of the changes made at Steps One and Two, you may need to seek employment elsewhere. Since changing your work didn't help, you'll have to consider changing jobs.

Step Three, therefore, calls for you to go back to the list you compiled at Step Two, describing the major aspects of your work. Which part or parts do you like best? You may not be able to arrange at your current firm to do more of what you most enjoy. But that doesn't mean you can't do it at another firm.

Many people are nicer to strangers than they are to their friends, whom they take for granted and treat indifferently. And some, carrying it a step further, are nicer to their friends than they are to their own families. Regardless of how many people behave that way in their personal lives, the number who behave that way in business is huge. They are substantially nicer to outsiders and prospective employees than they are to their current employees.

As a consequence, the kind of work you are looking for may be readily available from a new employer, but not from your present one. If you can't "shape your work" at your current job, don't despair. Shape it "before the job," instead of "on the job," and go looking for it.

Needless to say, it is always easiest if you can get your present boss to cooperate in a shaping effort. Fortunately, many supervisors proved themselves willing to do just that. But you have to ask. No one can offer you this one unless you tell them what you want. Moreover, you need to be as precise as possible. Make it quite clear that you're not merely looking to lighten your load, and then spell out the fact that area A interests you enough to want to do more of it, but area (or person) B is costing you your appetite for work altogether.

Nothing is worse than a vague complaint. It doesn't communicate very much in describing a problem to an auto mechanic or a doctor, and it is nearly useless when talking to your boss. Besides, you are going to wind up paying the mechanic or doctor to find out what ails you. So if it takes many hours or visits, that is OK with them. Your employer, on the other hand, is paying you, so you will have to accurately diagnose your own ills if you expect them to be remedied.

Even if your current boss is unwilling or (more frequently) unable to help you, the effort won't have been in vain. The time you spent clarifying in your own mind what you really want to do will be very useful in finding it elsewhere.

Remember, the change needn't be a drastic one to produce a significant improvement in your degree of satisfaction. That is especially important, since if you do indeed decide to switch to an entirely new field, you may well have to be prepared to start over again at the bottom. Rather than exposing yourself to so radical a demotion, the most effective alternative is a straightforward one: stay where you are, and start developing your skills in the area in which you would ultimately like to be active.

Step Four thus calls for you to look at your present position as merely providing a "bread-and-butter" source of income while you self-finance your growing involvement in another field. Consciously removing your emotional connection to your present job will help make it more bearable. Trying and not succeeding at improving it may have been adding substantially to the frustration you felt. If the situation is beyond saving, giving up—although hard to do—is the only realistic course of action.

A good rule of thumb for investing in yourself is: the more the work you like differs from that which you now do, the more probable it is that you will have to self-finance the transition to it. Often, though, the people in our sample who were unhappy with their work found that their interests lay in a related field. If that is so in your case, your employer may be willing to foot the bill for the retraining and experience you will need in order to begin doing full time the work you most enjoy.

QUESTION SEVENTEEN. I do want to make some changes, but something is stopping me. It's probably just laziness or habit, isn't it?

Maybe. But the single, greatest obstacle the people we studied encountered in attempting to find work they enjoyed was their own snobbery. They didn't prop a pinky in the air when they drank a martini, nor did they smoke cigarettes in a long holder and look down their nose at the great unwashed. But they were monumental snobs nonetheless. For they viewed almost every other kind of work—except the one they were presently doing—as being beneath them.

They rarely put it into words, knowing that they would offend someone if they did. But their disdain, although silent, was severely inhibiting. Switching to another field was going to entail more than just new knowledge and some practice. It wasn't going to be just a horizontal move to another office in another building. It was also going to involve a loss of status.

What, then, was the sense of making the move? It was going to be hard enough in any event to become adequately retrained and familiar with the everyday practices of a new field. There were also inevitably going to be some personal, financial, and perhaps even geographical sacrifices demanded by the switch. But to do all that and then be rewarded by a solid step down made the whole effort seem self-defeating.

The matter remained for the most part unconscious and hence not subject to scrutiny. But like all haughty airs, theirs was based on a fear of being found inferior. They rarely said it outright, yet they knew their snooty stance was based on a question which frightened them, one they would have been embarrassed to even utter: "What will people say?"

The question was such a cliché, they could ask it of themselves only mockingly, not seriously. But its effects were powerful and enduring. A radiologist who would have preferred being a tailor, a chemicals salesman who'd have preferred being a carpenter, and an English teacher who wanted to own a tavern all were crippled by the question.

It bothered both men and women, young and old, more than all the other factors combined: superiority and inferiority, an inescapable and immobilizing consideration. "I want to start a private mail service," said Andrea, who worked for a magazine and who was tired of hearing about the problems the post office was having. To some extent, it bothered her that her friends might label her, as she put it, "a mailwoman." But what disturbed her enormously more was that in her view the work was "low." Blue collar. Manual labor. Inferior. "Who delivers mail, anyway?" she asked, knowing very well what her answer would be. "Do you know what kind of people deliver mail?"

If you are still dissatisfied with your work after decisively attempting to shape it, then difficult as it will be, you'll somehow have to suspend your biases about what work is "high" and what is "low." If you are at all typical, there is one thing of which you may rest assured: it won't be easy.

One of the lasting consequences of sending every youngster to school, and telling them to stay there as many years as they can, is that a remarkable amount of snobbery accumulates little by little in their minds as to what kinds of work are suitable and what kinds are not. The overly academic curriculum they study can't help but prejudice them strongly against a wide variety of occupations in which they were given no training whatever. The intense emphasis upon preparing for professional, white-collar work eventually leads those who have accepted its primacy to paint themselves into a corner.

Once they have graduated and entered the work world, if they think about changing fields at all, their tremendous (hidden) snobbery guarantees that they will feel they have nowhere to go but down.

Well, what *will* people say if you are unhappy in one area and switch to another? Having examined a wide variety of such reactions with particular care, we can tell you that people will respond in an exceedingly simple way. Namely, if *you* are content with the choice, they too will be. But if you are at all uncomfortable about the social status your new line of work is accorded, they too will be disapproving. And the more discomfort you display, the more critical and condemnatory they are likely to be. Your friends will "read" your feelings surprisingly well in this matter and will act accordingly.

Of course, if you are discontent, you could always do what most of the people who are dissatisfied with their work do: pretend. Instead of acknowledging their unhappiness and subjecting themselves to the trauma of searching for work they enjoyed, they loudly claimed they had already found it. "I'm really into my work," they said. "Man, I'm really into it." Some put on extraordinarily convincing performances.

But after witnessing those performances over an extended period, it became apparent that the only thing they are really into is persuading you that they are really into something. What makes such behavior hilarious, if commonplace, is that the people who were so into their work they eventually became well known and wealthy as a result were likely to underplay rather than boast about their deep absorption in it. No one who really had it had to flaunt it.

There were others who were so competitive they never even stopped to think about whether or not they enjoyed what they were doing. As long as they were beating out or showing up someone else, they were happy. But ironically, that ultimately produced the reverse of the outcome they had hoped for. In the end, they usually commented, "I've achieved all this, and it doesn't mean anything to me."

Nothing is worse than succeeding at a business you don't particularly care for. Yet it happens frequently, because many have not had the good luck in the past to run into someone viciously competitive who bumped them out of the picture. Or else they themselves are viciously competitive and have spent their lives winning a prize they never really wanted. Struggling blinded them. Had they never succeeded, they'd never have noticed how little interest they had in their field.

It would be difficult to overestimate the importance of self-financing your involvement in work you enjoy, even if you like your current job. Only rarely did we find people who were being paid to do exactly what they wanted to do. And what characterized those who eventually became rich was their willingness to spend time and money pursuing on their own any aspect of their work they found fascinating.

No one knows what is going to be a resounding success next year, much less five, ten or twenty years from now. But twenty years ago those who allowed their interests to guide them, and who accidentally persisted until they developed great skill in the areas they enjoyed, were suddenly discovered by the world and catapulted to the forefront.

The whole system for determining who becomes rich and famous may strike you as remarkably random and haphazard. Yet it does indeed work, and works well, at that. In short, the only way you can find the wealth and recognition you seek is to not look for it. Because you will be basing your actions on today's successes, and what you really want is to be one of tomorrow's.

INDEX

ABOUT THE AUTHOR

Srully Blotnick did his graduate work at Berkeley and Princeton, where he was a National Science Foundation Fellow. He is a financial expert who has worked as Director of Research at several Wall Street brokerage houses. He currently heads his own consulting firm, has written a book on investing, and writes a regular column for *Forbes* magazine.